D0628244

Managing
Archival & Manuscript Repositories

Managing Archival and Manuscript Repositories
by Michael J. Kurtz

Arranging and Describing Archives and Manuscripts
by Kathleen D. Roe

Selecting and Appraising Archives and Manuscripts
by Frank Boles

Providing Reference Services for Archives and Manuscripts
by Mary Jo Pugh

Preserving Archives and Manuscripts
by Mary Lynn Ritzenthaler

Understanding Archives and Manuscripts
by James M. O'Toole & Richard J. Cox

A Glossary of Archival and Records Terminology
by Richard Pearce-Moses

Managing
Archival & Manuscript Repositories

Michael J. Kurtz

Chicago

The Society of American Archivists
527 S. Wells Street, 5th Floor
Chicago, IL 60607 USA
312/922-0140 Fax 312/347-1452
www.archivists.org

©2004 by the Society of American Archivists.
All Rights Reserved.

Library of Congress Cataloging-in-Publication Data
Kurtz, Michael J.
Managing archival & manuscript repositories / Michael J. Kurtz.
p. cm. -- (Archival fundamentals series. II)
Includes bibliographical references and index.
ISBN 1-931666-09-1
1. Archives--Administration. I. Title: Managing archival and manuscript repositories. II. Society of American Archivists. III. Title. IV. Series.

CD950.K87 2004
025.17'14--dc22

2004052468

Graphic design by Matt Dufek, dufekdesign@yahoo.com.
Fonts: Minion (text and footnotes); Meta (secondary text and captions).

Table *of* Contents

Preface to the ARCHIVAL FUNDAMENTALS SERIES II

There was a time when individuals entering the archives profession could read a few texts, peruse some journals, and attend a workshop and institute or two and walk away with a sense that they grasped the field's knowledge and discipline. This was an inadequate perception, of course, but it was true that the publications—basic or advanced, practical or theoretical—were modest in number.

The archival world has changed considerably since these more quiet times. A rich monographic research literature is developing. Scholars from far outside the field are examining the "archive" and the "record." Archives, archivists, records, and records managers are in the daily news as cases appear testing government and corporate accountability, organizational and societal memory, and the nature of documentary evidence emerge—all challenging basic archival work and knowledge.

The new edition of the Archival Fundamentals Series (AFS II) is intended to provide the basic foundation for modern archival practice and theory. The original preface (written by Mary Jo Pugh in her capacity as the series editor) to the first editions, which were published in the early to mid-1990s by the Society of American Archivists (SAA), argued that the seven volumes "have been conceived and written to be a foundation for modern archival theory and practice" and aimed at "archivists, general practitioners and specialists alike, who are performing a wide range of archival duties in all types of archival and manuscript repositories." It is hard to better state the purpose of the new AFS editions.

There are some differences, both subtle and obvious, in the new volumes. The new editions are more open-ended than earlier versions, extending back to the Basic Manual Series published a quarter-of-a-century ago by SAA, reflecting evolving viewpoints about archival theory and practice. Even more important a difference is the broader and deeper context of archival publishing AFS volumes reside in. Mary Jo Pugh, in her introduction of just a decade ago, noted that the AFS titles are companions to "more specialized manuals also available from SAA." Now, SAA has four other series (some just getting underway), including Archival Classics (featuring reprints or new collections of older publications with pivotal importance to the profession), Archival Readers (both collections of new and previously published essays intended to supplement the descriptions of foundational theory and practice of the AFS II volumes), International Archival Studies Readers (both collections of new and previously published essays intended to provide glimpses of archival work and knowledge outside of North America), and Archival Cases and Case Studies (examining archival work in a variety of institutional types and with a variety of media). Added to SAA's own publications is a vast sea of new titles pouring from the presses of other professional associations and trade, professional, and university publishers.

The particular value of both the Basic Manual and Archival Fundamentals Series is that they can provide a sort of benchmark in the development of archival knowledge and work. One can trace changing ideas and practices about archival description by reading the 1977, 1990, and 2004 volumes dedicated to this subject in the respective SAA manual series. One also expects to find in the more recent volume the current standards and consensus about this aspect of archival work. One also expects now, of course, that some will disagree with aspects of the current presentation, and there they can point to the growing research and case study literature being generated by the archival profession.

Many people participated in the production of the various volumes constituting the Archival Fundamentals Series II. The profession owes its gratitude not only to the authors, but to various chairs and members of the SAA Publications Board, Photo Editor for the series (Miriam Mieslik), the SAA Executive Directors (Susan Fox and Nancy P. Beaumont), and especially to Teresa Brinati, Director of Publishing at SAA, whose good humor, organization, and steady commitment to a quality product helped keep the publishing of these and other SAA volumes on track.

RICHARD J. COX
Publications Editor
Society of American Archivists

Introductory Note

This new edition of *Managing Archival and Manuscript Repositories* is being published almost twelve years after the original version written by Thomas Wilsted and William Nolte. I am in their debt, for a great deal of what they wrote is still relevant and has found its way into this edition. Yet the past decade has witnessed dramatic changes in management concepts and practice, organizational theory, and information technology. The archival profession is in the midst of profound change, and this manual reflects the transitional nature of the present era. New management paradigms influenced by expanding insights into group behavior and the relentless advances of information technology continue to reshape the workplace and how managers interact with their environment. The paradigm selected for this manual, organizational complexity, is one among many and will undoubtedly evolve rapidly into other theories and approaches. Changes in organizational theory, communications, information technology, and the increasingly complicated and sophisticated projects performed in the archival setting are reflected in this edition. The rapidity of change affecting the management of archival and manuscript repositories indicates, at least to me, the need for regularly scheduled updates to the manual. In this way, the most current management theories, concepts, and practices can be made available to the archival community in a timely manner. One method to consider for the future is an on-line publication that allows updates to be made selectively and on an as-needed basis.

This manual covers a wide variety of management tasks, responsibilities, and roles. It is not possible to cover any of the topics in enough depth to be comprehensive and all inclusive. Rather, the approach is to present a coherent and sensible narrative which provides the framework for understanding each issue in the archival context. Charts, forms, photographs, and other illustrations are designed to add substance to the narrative and to assist archival managers in performing their tasks. The footnotes, suggested readings at the end of each chapter, and the appendix on "Management Literature, Web Sites, and Professional Associations" will, hopefully, provide a roadmap for further study and learning.

I would like to conclude by expressing my sincere appreciation to those who reviewed the manual at various stages of development and provided insightful suggestions to improve the text and presentation. In particular, I would like to thank Kimberly Barata, a member of SAA's Publications Board, and others from the board who took the time and effort to provide detailed and constructive comments. I also want to express my deepest appreciation to Diana Matthis for all of her assistance in typing and preparing the manuscript. And I am grateful for the support and encouragement I received from Richard J. Cox, SAA's Publications Editor, and Teresa Brinati, Director of Publishing for SAA.

MICHAEL J. KURTZ
March 2004

Chapter 1

Management Theory and Practice

Many theorists and authors have described management and its attendant roles, responsibilities, and tasks. There are as many definitions of management as there are authors. For purposes of simplicity and clarity, let us use the definition provided in *Webster's Third New International Dictionary of the English Language* (1971 edition): "The executive function of planning, coordinating, directing, controlling, and supervising any industrial or business project or activity with responsibility for results." *Webster's* further defines management as, "The collective body of those who manage or direct any enterprise or interest." Thus, in two sentences we find the essential duties, identity, and purpose of management sketched out.

Noted management guru Peter Drucker feels that management is the key organ of any institution, responsible for the performance and very survival of the organization.[1] From the perspective of Drucker and others, the success of institutions, whether in the public or private sectors, depends upon the successful execution of management tasks and remaining focused on serving the core mission of the institution. Successful and functional institutions are the bedrock of society, and when institutions do deteriorate, often due to inept or dysfunctional management, society suffers. Such problems, if serious enough, can threaten the very foundations of our democratic society. So, manage-

1 Peter Drucker, *Management: Tasks, Responsibilities, Practices* (New York: Harper and Row, 1974), x.

ment effectiveness matters. It is not merely an extra set of duties thrown upon a busy professional. The art and science of management have their own values, theories, and practices. Whether one is the sole archival professional in a group or part of a larger archival enterprise, the work of management is critical for the success and survival of the archival program.

Though effective management is vitally important, too much management can be a hazard. Theories and approaches appropriate to the industrial age are increasingly perceived as outmoded and ineffective. Traditional command-and-control management structures are regarded as restrictive and antithetical to the creativity released through information technology, the employee's own performance and quality, and democratic trends in the workplace and in society. Too much management can be a deadweight, stifling productivity and creativity. Managers today are being trained and encouraged to lead through coaching and mentoring so that staff members, increasingly organized in less formal structures, can develop to their fullest potential. Such attitudes and approaches are liberating to the manager as well. Moving away from a routinized view of management roles, tasks, and responsibilities can stimulate the manager's own creativity and help sustain and nourish lifelong career development. Drucker's insights into the fundamentals of management lend themselves to a variety of forms, structures, and expression.

Modern Management

Management concepts and practice have evolved over time. The Mayan temples, the Great Wall of China, and the pyramids in Egypt each required management skill to build. Armies and empires throughout history have required the basic management skills of planning, organizing, and directing or leading to survive and flourish. Different eras of history such as the Renaissance, the scientific revolution, and the Enlightenment developed a variety of management practices to cope with evermore complex societies.

But management as a distinct discipline and identity began its modern evolution and development with the Industrial Revolution, particularly in the United States and western Europe. Peter Drucker, in fact, regards *management* as a uniquely American term describing a function, a group of specially tasked individuals, and a discrete field of study.[2]

The era of the Industrial Revolution coincided with an emphasis on science and scientific approaches to academic fields of study (e.g., history) and practical applications such as management. The first prominent American management theorist and practitioner was Frederick W. Taylor. Taylor, an engineer, sought to improve society and hold managers and workers accountable for performing a "fair day's work" through increased productivity and efficiency of the workforce. Though he stressed management research, training, and problem solving, Taylor's primary approach was the development of scientific, engineered work-measurement standards. This reflected both a scientific management approach and the reality of the mechanistic, assembly-line division of work characteristic of the modern industrial era.[3]

A contemporary of Taylor's, Belgian industrialist Henri Fayol believed that scientific management could be applied to other than industrial settings. Fayol identified five basic management functions—planning, organizing, budgeting, directing, and controlling—common to all organizations.[4] Though added to by later theorists, Fayol's functional delineation of management work has endured.[5] A reaction to Taylor and his followers began around World War I and continued for the next several decades. Focusing on human behavior and psychology, academics and management practitioners such as Elton Mayo, Hugo Munsterberg, and Mary Parker Follett, who wrote between the late 1920s and the early 1950s, sought to emphasize the worker's skills and need for autonomy, and the importance of viewing the workforce as a

2 Ibid., 5.

3 G. Edward Evans, Patricia Layzell Ward, and Bendik Rugaas, *Management Basics for Information Professionals* (New York and London: Neal-Schuman Publishers, Inc., 2000), 11.

4 Ibid., 19–20

5 In the 1930s, Luther Gulick expanded Fayol's categories and developed what he identified as POSDCORB, or Planning, Organizing, Staffing, Directing, Coordinating, Reporting, and Budgeting. A number of contemporary theorists, such as Henry Mintzberg, do not accept these categories as accurately reflecting management work. He emphasizes not the "functions" performed by managers, rather the "roles" played by managers in day-to-day work.

group and not just a collection of individuals.[6] This Human Relations School was succeeded by a generation of management thinkers such as Abraham Maslow, Douglas McGregor, and Chester Barnard in the 1950s, 1960s, and 1970s, and Peter Drucker, who wrote into the early 1990s. They built on the insights provided by psychology, sociology, and philosophy to explore motivation and organizational behavior.[7] Those theorists sought balance between the insights of earlier schools of thought and the dynamic changes affecting society and the workplace.

Though the basic tasks identified by Fayol continue to be relevant in managerial work, the past twenty-five years have seen new and potentially transformational management themes and approaches emerge which have changed the way people and organizations work. Total quality management, business process re-engineering, learning organizations, communities of practice, and knowledge management all contribute to the trend away from financial accounting as the principal focus of management to a deeper understanding of what constitutes value and sustainable organizational success. The information technology revolution, with its profound implications in the communications and knowledge arenas, has reshaped the focus of the contemporary manager. Intense competitive factors in the marketplace, the reinvention of government at all levels, and the demands of customers and citizens have driven the emphasis on quality and customers that consume the modern organization. Customer expectations are a major "driver" influencing all business and every organization. Customer needs influence services provided, the way such services are made available, quality requirements, and staff and unit performance standards. Customer expectations are such persuasive "drivers" that they influence every function discussed in this manual. One example among many is the adaptation of product plans from the information technology (IT) world for use in planning and designing customer-based products not necessarily IT-based. (See chapter 7, "Managing Information Technology.")

Knowledge management, though an emerging discipline with theory and practice in flux, is driven by the conviction that in this

---

6 Evans, Ward, and Rugaas, Management Basics, 13–14

7 Ibid., 17–18

Assisting a researcher at the University of Nevada Las Vegas. UNIVERSITY OF NEVADA LAS VEGAS.

information- and science-driven world, effectively managing organizational knowledge is essential to achieving organizational success. Author William Saffady defines knowledge management as the "systematic, effective management and utilization of an organization's knowledge resources. It encompasses the creation, storage, arrangement, retrieval, and distribution of an organization's knowledge."[8] The ways in which individuals can identify and acquire information and then the transformation of information into new knowledge are the keys to organizational success. The skills required in the knowledge management (KM) environment are a complex mix of the organizational-managerial and the professional and technical. (See figure 1-1.)

The needs to manage institutional knowledge and to develop strategies for developing and retaining knowledge affect organizations of every variety and size. A new tool in this endeavor that is attracting management attention is a phenomenon known as "communities of practice." These are "groups of people who share a set of

8 William Saffady, "Knowledge Management: An Overview," *The Information Management Journal* (July 2000): 4.

Figure 1-1

Skills for the KM Environment

- KM enabling skills and competencies
- Business process identification and analysis
- Understanding the knowledge process within the business process
- Understanding the value context, and dynamics of knowledge and information
- Knowledge of mapping and flows
- Change management
- Leveraging ICT to create KM enablers
- An understanding of support and facilitation of communities and teams
- Project management
- Information structuring and architecture
- Document and information management and work flows
- An understanding of information management principles
- An understanding of publishing process
- An understanding of technological opportunities
- Professional, technical, and craft skills and education

Core Competency Building

Continuing professional and technical education and training

Business, sector, and work experience

Organizational skills and competencies

>Communications
>Team working
>Negotiation
>Persuasion
>Facilitation
>Coaching
>Mentoring
>Business process

(Courtesy of The Informational Management Journal. *This chart appeared in the July 2000 issue in an article by Angela Abell, "Skills for Knowledge Environments.")*

problems, or a passion about a topic, and who deepen their knowledge and expertise in the area by interacting on an on-going basis."[9] Managers need to support these informal groups, which can operate within a unit or across an organization, in an effort to develop and share knowledge and to generate new approaches to work outside the confines of bureaucratic structure. Knowledge management and communities of practice will be discussed in more detail in subsequent chapters in this manual.

From all this research and experience, managers today have a far better idea of how organizational systems actually function, what motivates employees, and the critical, unifying role of management in the entire equation. The application of management skills in the archival context is our focus throughout this manual.

The Archival Context

Management is basically about people, what they do, and the organizations in which they work. From that perspective, an archives is like any other organization. The archives has its mission-related tasks to perform requiring the judicious application of available resources (i.e., money, people, space, and equipment). Much of what is discussed in the chapters of this manual reflects basic management tasks carried out in a variety of organizational frameworks and settings.

The archival manager, however, faces certain challenges particular to the archival environment. Most archival operations are small (sometimes only one "lone arranger") and are located within larger, parent institutions whose primary mission is usually not related to records. Questions of value to the organization and cost effectiveness are paramount. Rapid changes in information technology are profoundly altering work processes, communication systems and methods, and how business is conducted. Major changes in how records are created, used, and preserved affect archival operations in almost all institutional settings.

---

9 E. Wenger, R. McDermott, and W. Snyder, *Cultivating Communities of Practice: A Guide to Managing Knowledge* (Harvard Business School: Boston, Massachusetts, 2002), 4.

Many archival programs operate in the corporate sector where restructuring and downsizing are hallmarks of the contemporary scene. Changes are prevalent in other sectors, nonprofit and government, as well. The need for adding value, costs, and information technology is a tremendous force for change. The archival manager, regardless of the size of the program, must understand the key tasks for which he or she is responsible and have the necessary skills to perform the job. In the extremely competitive environment in which most archival programs operate today, poor management quite possibly means doom. Management skills can be gained through a combination of education, training, on-the-job experience, and motivation.

Archivists are educated and trained first and foremost to be archivists. In small operations management is an ancillary task, and in larger organizations a management position is a step up the career ladder. Because management is a separate field of study and discipline, most archivists in positions of management have received little or no relevant education or training. Managers, like other professionals, are not born. Rather, their skills are developed through education, training courses, mentoring, and on-the-job experience. Managers, newly minted or experienced, must have the motivation to get the professional education, training, or continuing education needed to develop and sustain their ability to meet their responsibilities. Management tasks are demanding, often complex, and critical to the survival of the archival program.

A section on "Management Literature, Web Sites, and Professional Associations" at the end of this manual provides sources for archival managers seeking to strengthen their management skills and abilities. Journals and other literature on-line enable the busy manager to skim, select what is useful, and then absorb. Seminars and workshops offered by professional archival associations, business schools, and community colleges, or through the workplace offer the opportunity for concentrated learning and interacting with other management professionals. If time and resources permit, extended participation in programs offered by various management institutes could definitely broaden a manager's horizons.

Roles and Responsibilities

Boiled down to the essence, the roles and responsibilities of management are basically the same regardless of type of institution. Institutional missions and cultures, of course, vary widely, but there are core tasks and duties that come with management wherever and whatever the setting. All managers perform their work within a system and, in fact, manage systems. Simply put, systems comprise patterns of behavior repeated over time reflective of the natural and social orders. For example, human beings have nervous-muscular patterns from which systems—nervous, digestive, and cardiac—are formed. Similarly, repeated patterns of social behavior lead to different systems such as political, educational, business, or cultural. Systems are interdependent (i.e., organs of the body) and reflect their environment. A key factor for all systems is that change is difficult. Inertia is the norm. This can be helpful or not depending on circumstances.

So, managers are always operating within and managing a variety of organizational systems and subsystems. Access, for example, is one of several systems operating in the archival environment. This system, which enables researchers and others to use the holdings, interacts with other systems (e.g., preservation, administration) and has its own subsystems (i.e., description, collections management, reference). Within broader system parameters, managers have a variety of roles and responsibilities. To a greater or lesser extent, each manager has multiple roles. Certainly the primary role is directing the unit in carrying out daily operations. But this deceptively simple definition masks other roles that must be successfully carried out if the directing role is to be accomplished.

The manager is a negotiator seeking resources for the program, working out arrangements with other units or outside groups, and gaining the support of the staff. The manager is also a planner looking at short-, mid-, and long-term threats and opportunities and devising strategies to maximize operational potential to meet mission objectives. Along these lines the manager must also have an innovative or entrepreneurial bent that can turn threats into opportunities. Or as the old saying goes, be able to "make lemonade out of lemons."

The manager needs to train and develop staff, volunteers, and others who interact with the program, playing, in essence, the role of nurturer. Among other skills, this means learning to carefully listen to others with an open mind (see chapter 9 on communication). What many managers may not realize is that success on the job is in good measure a reflection of their personal development as human beings. The more well rounded an individual, the more likely professional satisfaction is achieved.

The responsibilities or tasks of the manager reflect the evolution of management practice and theory since the Industrial Revolution. These include everything from planning for the organization, creating an effective organizational structure for mission performance, and hiring and directing qualified staff for the important but often little-recognized task of managing archival facilities. (See chapter 10.) A major function is coordination. In managing a system and interacting with other systems, effective coordination is vital. Coordination and its partner communication are the grease needed to keep people working together and focused on completing tasks or projects in a timely and effective fashion. Coordination and communication are the tools needed by the manager so that the resources of the organization (e.g., money, people, and facilities) can be effectively integrated in carrying out managerial functions. (See figure 1-2.)

Another important management responsibility is budgeting. The ability not only to obtain resources but to manage and expend them so that program goals are achieved is a major building block for organizational success. Last but not least, in a systems environment, reporting or feedback is a key loop. Supervisors, colleagues, staff, and customers all need to know what is happening in the program. Regardless of format (narrative or statistical, automated or hard copy) reporting is needed to ascertain whether the program is meeting its goals and objectives, whether funds are being properly expended, and if problems or issues that need to be confronted are looming.

A great deal in management literature identifies and analyzes various management styles. Perhaps the basic point to understand is that a particular managerial style most likely reflects an organization's culture. Again, turning to *Webster's,* the word *culture* is defined as "a complex of typical behaviors or standardized social characteristics peculiar to a specific group, occupation, or profession, sex, age, or grade."

Figure 1-2 Resources and the Managerial Functions

FUNCTION:	Planning	Organizing	Staffing	Directing	Controlling
RESOURCE:					
Money	Organization's master planning (covers all resources)	Multiyear financial plan	Selection, training, motivation	Periodic accounting data	Budgets
People		Hiring		Meetings, written communication	Performance review
Facilities		Blueprints, building plans		Repair orders	Maintenance logs

Some organizational cultures value aggressive and innovative managers, while others value consistency, stability, and the maintenance of the status quo. There are organizational cultural differences between public or private sector institutions, industry, small business, and cultural organizations. A manager, particularly a prospective one, should attempt to understand an institution's culture, particularly its management ethos, to determine if his or her style (reflective of the individual's own values, experience, and personality) meshes with the culture of the organization.

This is not an easy task. Organizational culture is often unstated and reflects years of institutional trial and error in working out solutions to recurring issues or situations, sometimes documented in policies and procedures and sometimes not. It's "how we do things here" and how the group looks at the world. A manager's style has to be in sync with the organizational culture for the manager to be fully effective. If it is not, then at least the manager must understand the organizational environment to develop effective coping strategies.

Roles and responsibilities for archival managers have been profoundly affected by the information revolution. The information revolution has forced managers to compete for functional identity. Ask most executives to whom they could turn for advice on dealing with rare, old records, and "an archivist" would probably be a reassuringly high response. Ask the same executives to whom they would turn to ensure that a new information system can store and retrieve records over an extended period of time, and the number answering "an archivist" would probably fall. Another impact to keep in mind is that changes in information technology erode the traditional divisions between the information professions. Librarians, archivists, and other information professionals must face those factors stimulating competition and change to adapt and survive. Both of these key issues are discussed in chapter 7, Managing Information Technology.

Administrative Competence

Those who seek to succeed in management require basic administrative competence. Archival managers must organize the paperwork that flows across the desk or the computer if they wish to use their time most efficiently. This requires a well-organized filing system so that material is filed and retrieved in an expeditious manner. In addition to subject files, the archivist should have a bring-up or "tickler" system where letters requiring a follow-up response are filed. Arranged on a monthly basis for the upcoming twelve months, it can be subdivided by days for the current month. Such a system will ensure adequate follow-up to acquisition requests or other letters that require a response. This system can be automated or manual, as long as it is one the manager can use.

Many archivists have responsibility for records management within their parent institutions. In developing record retention schedules and procedures, the archives' own records should not be overlooked. Inactive records should be regularly removed from active files. Scheduled records should be retired as soon as the retention date has been reached, and archival managers should also apply other records management techniques, such as forms and files management, to their own records.

Archival managers can reduce the volume of correspondence by using e-mail and the telephone, by delegating the work, or by using personalized form letters. Word processing aids in composing form paragraphs for a variety of letters and can save considerable time in acknowledging donations or answering reference questions. Fax machines, teleconferencing, and video-conferencing are all tools that can assist in the management of unavoidable administrative work and in that most essential leadership task, communication.

Archival managers must make every effort to conserve their time. One method is careful evaluation of voluntary tasks, such as professional responsibilities, internal working groups, or task forces. Although such tasks are sometimes required, archival administrators often have a choice of whether or not to assume responsibility for a specific job. When that is the case, the archival administrator should carefully evaluate whether assuming responsibility will assist or hinder personal or institutional goals and make an appropriate decision. In addition to reviewing whether or not a task supports institutional or personal goals, archival administrators must also ensure that they do not take on more tasks than it is possible to complete. Not only is such action irresponsible, but there is every likelihood that the tasks will be done poorly, if at all.

Time Management

Time is perhaps the most important resource archivists possess. Archives are labor intensive; many do not require the latest high-technology equipment, expensive laboratories, or design studios. Their primary needs are space and time: time to identify and acquire, time to process, time to conserve, and time to provide reference services.

In carrying out managerial tasks, archivists must ensure that their time and their employees' time are used to achieve the repository's goals. Archivists faced with an overwhelming number of tasks and only a finite amount of time to complete them can only accomplish them by

- Spending more time at work;
- Doing work more quickly or efficiently;
- Delegating work to others, including paraprofessional staff;
- Eliminating tasks that do not lead to the achievement of archival goals.

To spend time more wisely, archivists must organize themselves for the day, the week, the month, and the year by establishing both institutional and personal goals. After such goals have been set, archivists must evaluate how their time is spent and whether it is actively used to achieve goals.

Completing a time log is one of the most common ways managers evaluate their use of time. Such logs record the time of day and the type of activity and its duration, and they allow managers to rate that activity in relation to personal and institutional goals. To evaluate the use of time, the archival manager should complete a time log on a periodic basis. Such a time log should be kept over three to ten workdays, preferably during a period when the archivist is carrying out normal duties. When the log is complete, the archivist must evaluate how the time was spent. Did the activities lead toward personal or institutional goals? Was time wasted on activities that could have been done by someone else or not done at all? Such an evaluation will assist the archivist in revising patterns of behavior that are not goal oriented so that time can be used to maximum advantage. (See figure 1-3.)

Making the best use of personal time also implies self-understanding. The archivist should rank tasks in order of importance, attending to the highest priority tasks first. If writing is an important aspect of one's work, it should be scheduled at a time of greatest effectiveness. For many, this is early in the morning, while others can write late into the night. Individuals must evaluate their own personality and working situation so as to use time effectively to achieve both personal and institutional goals.

Conclusion

A key role mixed in with all the other managerial roles and functions is that of leader. Leadership is a complex topic more fully discussed in the next chapter. Suffice it to say, the roles of manager and leader are inextricably linked. It is not an either/or situation, but a both/and proposition. Without leadership skills the manager most likely will not succeed. Leadership and management skills go hand-in-hand for the successful archival administrator. The ability to organize, plan, budget, and develop staff are key management tasks and responsibilities that the archival manager must master. The combination of these management skills, along with the vision and purpose of leadership, is the goal sought by conscientious managers over the length of busy and productive careers. The chapters that follow are dedicated to assisting in the development of the management and leadership skills required for a successful career in archival management.

Suggested Readings

A very useful source for managers in all aspects of information services (including archives) is G. Edward Evans, Patricia Layzell Ward, Bendik Rugaas, *Management Basics for Information Professionals* (New

Figure 1-3 Time Log

Priority Rating
1. Important and urgent 2. Important, not urgent 3. Routine 4. Not business related

Monday, June 1

Time	Activity	Duration	Priority	Comments
8 a.m.	Long-range plan	15 minutes	1	
8:15	Phone call	15 minutes	2	Boss calling to discuss employee annual review.
8:30	Long-range plan	30 minutes	1	
9:00	Staff meeting	75 minutes	3	Meeting dragged on too long, people wouldn't stick to the agenda. Reference archivist wanted to discuss personal issues that were inappropriate.
10:15	Coffee	15 minutes	3	
10:30	Meeting with mobile shelving representative	30 minutes	2	Discussed shelving specifications for new addition
11:00	Long-range plan	10 minutes	1	
11:10	Husband called	15 minutes	4	
11:25	Colleague called	40 minutes	3	Called about a reference for a former employee
12:05	Lunch	40 minutes	3	

York and London: Neal-Schuman Publishers, Inc., 2000). This text covers all aspects of management work, beginning with an excellent summary of "Management Concepts" in chapter 1.

Henry Mintzberg, *The Nature of Managerial Work* (New York: Harper and Row, 1973), is a standard introduction to management—with emphasis on the subject of what managers actually do—and has influenced any number of subsequent works. Also, Peter Drucker, *Management: Tasks, Responsibilities, and Practice* (New York: Harper, 1974), is another standard text, with an emphasis on the critical importance of effective management for long-term societal health.

Two works on organizational culture, though somewhat dated, remain useful: Joseph A. Raelin, *The Clash of Cultures* (Boston: Harvard Business School Press, 1986); and Terrence E. Deal and Allen A. Kennedy, *The Rites and Rituals of Corporate Life* (Reading, Mass: Addison-Wesley, 1982).

For a focus on the nonprofit sector side of management, Peter Drucker, *Managing the Non-Profit Organization: Practices and Principles* (New York: Harper-Collins Publishers, 1990), is both entertaining and informative.

Chapter 2

Leadership in Management

In a rapidly changing and competitive environment, standards of performance of every organization must be raised, and that improving the quality of leadership is essential in raising these standards. [1]

—Harold K. Skramstad, Jr.

In this manual, a variety of management skills, abilities, and knowledge will be explored and analyzed. Like every other manager, the archival manager has a host of roles, functions, and responsibilities that need to be successfully carried out. The fundamental skill or ability that the manager must possess is leadership. The quality of leadership, as Harold Skramstad's quote indicates, is the essential ingredient for success. What constitutes leadership and its relationship to management tasks and responsibilities are often not clearly conceptualized or enunciated. Yet, most people would acknowledge that effective leadership, however defined, is critical for institutional success. Contemporary society is undergoing a vast transformation as we move from the industrial era to an information- and technology-based arena. Complex sociological and cultural phenomena are steadily changing the most fundamental ways institutions view their

1 Bryant F. Tolles, Jr., ed., *Leadership for the Future: Changing Directional Roles in American History Museums and Historical Societies* (Nashville, Tenn.: American Association for State and Local History, 1991), 23.

mission, organize for work, and relate to staff. Leaders in all sectors—corporate, government, and nonprofit—face major challenges.

A multicultural, diverse, and increasingly informed society demands flexible, responsive leadership. Bureaucratic and authoritarian styles of leadership are increasingly outmoded and ineffective. Poor performance, scandals, and other institutional failures are usually attributed to poor leadership. The American military is often considered the exception. Having struggled for decades with issues of merit and opportunity, the military puts a premium on effective leadership to ensure a strong focus on mission, performance, and retaining support from civilian society. While the archival manager is not a platoon leader or battalion commander, leadership skills are just as important in the archival setting as in any other sector in society. How does one become a leader? Is it an innate trait or a learned skill?

Innate or Learned?

A century or more ago, British historian Thomas Carlyle propounded the "Great Man" theory of history. The idea that leadership is reserved to those born with certain personality or character traits is now discredited, but there is a continuing debate whether leadership skills and management skills are really quite distinct from the perspectives of personality, skill sets, and function.

Abraham Zaleznik, a professor of management at Harvard Business School, believes that leaders and managers are basically different types of individuals. They differ in what motivates them, their personal history, and how they think and act. Organizations, according to Zaleznik, are either managerial or entrepreneurial in nature. Managerial cultures emphasize conflict resolution through compromise and operate within traditional modes of decision making, goal setting, and organizational relationships. Basically, managers preserve the status quo and run bureaucracies.[2] Zaleznik sees leaders arising in entrepreneurial organizational cultures that value risk-taking, operate

2 Abraham Zaleznik, "Managers and Leaders: Are They Different?" *Harvard Business Review: On Management* (New York: Harper and Row, 1995), 162–79.

outside the traditional chain of command, and emphasize close bonds between leader and staff. Leaders, unlike managers, do not operate top-down hierarchical operations. The emphasis is on change, creating opportunities, and forging strong personal relationships with mentors and staff. Zaleznik sees managers and leaders as coming from different environments with little to no cross-over between them.[3]

Henry Mintzberg, on the other hand, sees the role of leader as being one of what he terms the "interpersonal roles of the manager." As the individual heading a unit or program, the manager, by definition, has the role and responsibility of leadership as well. In breaking away from Henri Fayol's functional model, Mintzberg views the manager as performing three types of roles—interpersonal, decisional, and informational—often simultaneously in the course of carrying out the job. But leadership is inextricably part of the manager's work.[4]

Most management theorists and practitioners today believe that leadership is a skill that can be developed, and that it is a requirement for a successful and effective manager. It is true that some individuals are gifted with the ability to communicate, influence other peoples' opinions, and exert authoritative decision making. But leaders and managers are not different beings from different planets. Rather, effective management has leadership skills and abilities at its core. Not all individuals are singled out as leaders, but nearly everyone has some leadership skills that can be developed. It is also true that not everyone in authority necessarily has leadership skills. The position does not endow the incumbent with leadership ability. Only education, training, practice, and motivation foster leadership.

Many positions in a bureaucracy receive their power or authority from their rank rather than from the individual's particular skill as a leader. Such legitimized authority is given to department heads, church bishops, or publicly elected officials. That such individuals have power does not necessarily ensure that they can lead, and their failure often contributes to stagnation or institutional collapse. As managers, archivists have such legitimized authority. To use this

---

3 Ibid.

4 Henry Mintzberg, "The Manager's Job: Folklore and Fact," *Harvard Business Review: On Management* (New York: Harper and Row, 1995), 104–24.

power to lead, however, managers must develop leadership skills that take them beyond the authority to make decisions. (See figure 2-1.)

Vision, Leadership, and Goals

One of the most important components of leadership is vision, the ability to imagine the results of both individual and group efforts. Skilled archival administrators envision what their repositories will achieve in one, five, and ten years. While the roadmap to this achievement is an archival plan, the image exists before the plan is drafted. Like plans, visions are not static. A vision can be affected by outside factors and must reflect current realities. An archival administrator's breadth and depth of both experience and training affect his or her vision. Archivists who have seen a wide variety of arrangement techniques or reference situations are better able to envision how they will carry out these tasks than someone who is inexperienced or who has experience in only one repository. People with vision have a broad perception of their role in the archives; the visions of leaders and managers are ultimately blended together to form the organization's vision expressed in a strategic or long-range plan.

Archival managers are responsible for mobilizing resources of the repository, the parent organization, and outside sources to achieve specific goals. To accomplish this, archivists must use leadership skills to influence a variety of groups and individuals both within and outside the repository.

Archival managers must begin by believing in themselves and the goals they set for their institutions. Too many archivists in small repositories either do not have specific goals or do not believe strongly enough in them to fight, argue, or cajole others into supporting the archival program. Managers in larger institutions must influence the archival staff, getting members to agree on goals and plans and devising work plans to achieve them. Whether working in a single-person archives or one with many staff members, the manager must believe in the cause and lead others to believe as well. In the contemporary era, the manager must exercise leadership to encourage team work, collaboration, and a more flexible organization. The manager must

Figure 2-1 Archival Leadership Skills

1. Leaders develop the team concept, choosing people with varying talents and allowing them to do what they do best, while simultaneously moving them toward an assigned goal.
2. Leaders think of renewal, developing strong values, new skills, and new leaders within the staff.
3. Leaders have good motivational skills and encourage their subordinates.
4. Leaders have good political skills and are able to resolve or reconcile conflicts and satisfy constituencies both inside and outside the repository.
5. Leaders seek to influence people outside the archives. They communicate not only the archives' intrinsic importance and purpose, but also its value to the larger organization.
6. Leaders see difficult situations not as problems, but as opportunities for seeking solutions.
7. Leaders are calm in the face of adversity. When faced with a challenge, they look for solutions rather than scapegoats.

help build a "nimble" organization, able to creatively respond to challenges and opportunities.

To be successful, the archival manager must identify the individuals critical to success and seek their support for the archives' goals. These persons include the leaders of the parent institution, immediate superiors, peers in other departments, subordinates, donors, researchers, and the general public. Each group looks at the repository from a different perspective, and the archival leader must use different methods to gain their support.

After identifying those constituencies critical to the success of the program, managers must define strategies to gain support for the goals. Archivists can assess the perceptions and motivations of different constituencies, appealing for their support and developing a stronger following for the archives. Only when a manager combines leadership skills, a strong will to achieve, and the ability to clearly define goals will real archival progress be made. There are many reasons why people support a particular program or person. Some of these include

- A record of success. If an individual or institution has been successful in achieving substantive goals or concrete results, people will be more likely to give their support. Has the manuscript repository acquired significant collections that have brought prestige or fame to the parent institution? Does the repository have a reputation for meeting the deadlines of the parent institution's administrators and staff?
- A belief in expertise. Specialists such as archivists can gain support because of their perceived special abilities or knowledge. Such support can be enhanced by a strong professional reputation or visible achievements in professional organizations.
- A belief in the repository's mission. People who have been closely involved with the repository as donors or researchers will have a better understanding of its role in preservation and research and are more likely to support its program.

The support of a variety of constituencies is critical to the archives' success in achieving its goals. However, without the leadership and vision of the archival manager, these groups cannot be organized and directed toward a common purpose.

Sharing the Vision

A leader, figuratively speaking, opens the doors to the archives and shares the records and staff expertise with others. An effective leader and manager is not just maintaining the status quo, but also is strengthening the archives for all those who need it. An archival manager must communicate the vision effectively and efficiently to each constituency. In addition to reviewing the use of personal time, archival managers must develop patterns of communication and work that increase their efficiency. Communication can range from a memorandum to a newsletter to an Internet or intranet announcement, and from brief one-on-one discussions to large staff meetings lasting hours. Archival managers should always choose the means of communication that shares the vision with the least amount of effort.

The organization's vision must be shared with the parent institution, resource allocators, research constituencies, and the general public. The manager needs to develop an effective communications style to successfully present the archival program and its vision to a variety of audiences. Good communication skills are important elements in leadership. Learning to give effective presentations may involve taking public presentation courses, joining organizations such as Toastmasters, or mastering PowerPoint technology. Written communications are just as important in effectively presenting the vision as those made orally. Taking refresher courses in grammar or writing may help to reinforce the ability to stay focused in presenting the vision. A leader must be able to share the vision if people are to be inspired and motivated to respond. (See figure 2-2.)

Figure 2-2 Vision

1. Leaders develop a vision of what they want to achieve as individuals.
2. Leaders develop a clear understanding of the parent institution, an appreciation of the role the repository plays within the institution, and a vision of what the archives should achieve.
3. Leaders have a vision of the goals of the profession and can adjust their institutional vision to support and enhance those goals.
4. Leaders have a clear understanding of the parent institution's history and culture and are able to assist their parent institution in developing a vision of the future based upon past achievements.
5. Having a vision of the future, archival leaders have the ability to select courses of action that will lead to those goals, rejecting or delaying tasks that can be done at some future date.

Self-Knowledge

A key factor in developing leadership skills is the critical faculty known as self-awareness or self-knowledge. To be effective managers, archivists must understand themselves. As individuals, archivists must assess their personal abilities and personality traits, and the effectiveness of their interaction with superiors, peers, and subordinates. Self-understanding is problematic at best. Individual perception of one's strengths and abilities can be quite different from those of colleagues, coworkers, and friends. If individuals are to succeed as archival managers, they must constantly test their perception of individual strengths and weaknesses against assessments made by others.

Individuals have specific personality traits. One may be an extrovert or an introvert, critical or supportive, sympathetic or indifferent. By developing a knowledge of one's strengths and weaknesses, the archival administrator can better relate to others. An introvert may take a public speaking course to encourage confidence, while someone who feels they are overly critical may make a strong effort to develop a more positive, supportive demeanor when dealing with staff members. Without making an effort to know oneself, such steps cannot be taken. An understanding of personal traits allows the archival administrator to carry out tasks more successfully. For example, an administrator who is not detail oriented may seek assistants with such skills to balance the management team. Archival administrators must continually evaluate their personal abilities and use such knowledge in the selection and promotion of other staff members.

Archivists must also develop an understanding of their professional skills and career goals. What is most important in a job—administering an interesting collection or solving an unusual set of administrative tasks? Is recognition by professional peers important? What types of archival tasks are the most interesting? Which tasks bring the greatest success? Is being a mid-level administrator in a large repository more satisfying than having full administrative responsibility in a small archives? Is one's strength in technical areas, such as arrangement and description, or in dealing with people in reference or archival acquisition? Is the individual detail oriented or more concerned with the larger picture?

Archival administrators must also be aware of their personal managerial style. Do they tend to be more collegial or authoritarian in their approach? What type of management style is prevalent within the parent institution? Management style can be an important issue, and clashes between individuals with an authoritarian style in a collegial environment and a collegial style in an authoritarian institution are not uncommon. Avoiding such problems requires archival administrators either to be flexible in their approach or to seek employment in an institution with a comparable management style.

The search for self-knowledge is continuous, and there are never simple answers or solutions. Archival managers will gain more personal satisfaction and achieve greater success if they develop an understanding of their personal and professional motivations. Such an understanding will allow decisions to be based on real needs and will assist the archival administrator in making choices based on reason rather than intuition.

Developing Leadership Skills

An important element in self-knowledge is understanding our preferences and aversions. A leader's grasp of this dynamic can elevate what can become destructive name calling and labeling into a constructive, organized system for understanding differences in human behavior and personality. This approach is based on the work of famed psychiatrist Carl Jung, later codified by Katherine Briggs and Isabel Briggs Myers into a psychological testing instrument known as the Myers-Briggs Type Indicators. This has become one of the basic tools used in developing awareness about differences in behavior, personal performance, and leadership stages.[5] The Myers-Briggs test is offered in countless seminars and workshops and by most human resources departments. This tool, along with others such as situational leadership and coaching, are extremely useful in understanding one's own preferences and aversions as well as those of others working as a team or in a unit. Utilizing this testing instrument early in one's career is highly recommended.

5 Otto Kroeger and Janet M. Thuesen, *Type Talk at Work* (New York: Dell Publishing, 1992), 6–7.

Another constructive, systematic way to develop leadership skills is through what recent research has defined as "emotional intelligence." Author Daniel Goleman defines it this way: "Emotional Intelligence—The ability to manage ourselves and our relationships effectively—consists of four fundamental capabilities: self-awareness, self management, social awareness, and social skill."[6] According to Goleman, each capability has a defined set of competencies that require nurturing and development. (See figure 2-3.) The research of Goleman and others defines six leadership styles that come from different components of emotional intelligence. These are coercive (immediate compliance); affiliative (forging emotional bonds and harmony); authoritative (mobilizing others toward a vision); democratic (building consensus through participation); pacesetting (excellence and self-direction); and coaching (developing people for the future). (See figure 2-4.)[7] Effective leaders focused on getting results must develop the ability to use the various styles as circumstances require.

This is a difficult challenge for any leader. In addition to psychological testing instruments, the leader seeking to broaden his or her range should work with a senior manager who can provide needed mentoring or coaching. The first step is to undergo what is known as a "360-degree evaluation" based on the competencies and components in emotional intelligence. This evaluation is performed by the individual's superiors, subordinates, and outside interlocutors, hence the title. Based on the results of the evaluation, the coach and the evaluatee develop a plan to address identified weaknesses and shortcomings. Then, over the period of months, the leader practices new behaviors in different work situations until the needed competencies are mastered.[8] This is hard going but necessary to increase the leader's portfolio of skills.

---

6 David Goleman, "Leadership That Gets Results," *Harvard Business Review* 78, no. 2, (March–April 2000): 80.

7 Ibid.

8 Ibid., 88–89.

Figure 2-3 Emotional Intelligence

Self-Awareness	Self-Management	Social Awareness	Social Skill
• *Emotional self-awareness:* the ability to read and understand your emotions as well as recognize their impact on work performance, relationships, and the like. • *Accurate self-assessment:* A realistic evaluation of your strengths and limitations. • *Self-confidence:* a strong and positive self-worth.	• *Self-control:* the ability to keep disruptive emotions and impulses under control. • *Trustworthiness:* a consistent display of honesty and integrity. • *Conscientiousness:* the ability to manage yourself and your responsibilities. • *Adaptability:* skill at adjusting to changing situations and overcoming obstacles.	• *Empathy:* skill at sensing other people's emotions, understanding their perspective, and taking an active interest in their concerns. • *Organizational awareness:* the ability to read the currents of organizational life, build decision networks, and navigate politics.	• *Visionary leadership:* the ability to take charge and inspire with a compelling vision. • *Influence:* the ability to wield a range of persuasive tactics. • *Developing others:* the propensity to bolster the abilities of others through feedback and guidance. • *Communication:* skill at listening and at sending clear, convincing, and well-tuned messages.

(continued)

Figure 2-3 continued

Self-Management	Social Awareness	Social Skill
• *Achievement orientation:* the drive to meet an internal standard of excellence. • *Initiative:* a readiness to seize opportunities.	• *Service orientation:* the ability to recognize and meet customers' needs.	• *Change catalyst:* proficiency in initiating new ideas and leading people in a new direction. • *Conflict management:* the ability to de-escalate disagreements and orchestrate resolutions. • *Building bonds:* proficiency at cultivating and maintaining a web of relationships. • *Teamwork and collaboration:* competence at promoting cooperation and building teams

Courtesy of the Harvard Business Review, *found in Daniel Goleman, "Leadership That Gets Results," vol. 78, no. 2 [March–April 2000], 80)*

Figure 2-4 The Six Leadership Styles

	Coercive	Authoritative	Affiliative
The leader's modus operandi	Demands immediate compliance	Mobilizes people toward a vision	Creates harmony and builds emotional bonds
The style in a phrase	"Do what I tell you."	"Come with me."	"People come first."
Underlying emotional intelligence competencies	Drive to achieve, initiative, self-control	Self-confidence, empathy, change catalyst	Empathy, building relationships, communication
When the style works best	In a crisis, to kick start a turnaround, or with problem employees	When changes, new vision, or when a direction is needed	To heal rifts in a team or to motivate people during stressful circumstances
Overall impact on climate	Negative	Most strongly positive	Positive

(continued)

Figure 2-4 continued

	Democratic	Pacesetting	Coaching
The leader's modus operandi	Forges consensus through participation	Sets high standards for performance	Develops people for the future
The style in a phrase	"What do you think?"	"Do as I do, now."	"Try this."
Underlying emotional intelligence competencies	Collaboration, team leadership, communication	Conscientiousness, drive to achieve, initiative	Developing others, empathy, self-awareness
When the style works best	To build buy-in or consensus, or to get input from valuable employees	To get quick results from a highly motivated and competent team	To help an employee improve performance or develop long-term strengths
Overall impact on climate	Positive	Negative	Positive

Courtesy of the Harvard Business Review, *found in Daniel Goleman, "Leadership That Gets Results," vol. 78, no. 2 [March–April 2000], 82–83)*

Mentoring

One of the responsibilities of leadership is to serve as a mentor for others in the organization. The archival manager is responsible not only for his or her own self-knowledge and development, but also for the development of leadership and management skills of subordinates on the staff. The most important way that this is done is by example. An organized, competent, and effective manager who focuses on the needs of the organization and of the staff becomes a model of professional leadership. Attention to big-picture issues as well as to routine management chores, such as timely and accurate personnel performance appraisals, demonstrates how a concerned manager operates.

Mentoring includes assisting employees in developing individual development plans for professional growth and advancement. Where appropriate, these plans or strategies would have leadership and management components. The mentoring manager should identify training courses or educational programs that will help employees develop leadership and management skills. Training assignments in other parts of the organization, as well as allowing staff members to "shadow" managers to observe firsthand the duties and responsibilities of management, for example, may be parts of a mentoring effort.

The archival manager should work with the institution's human resources department to utilize existing mentoring programs or to develop one if needed. Management competency is not a gift. It is a set of skills developed over time through education, training, and experience. Part of any good manager's legacy is leaving behind competent leadership to assume the responsibilities of management.

Conclusion

Leadership and management are not distinct and separate skill sets. There must be leadership *in* management. Every successful leader must be able to plan, organize, and direct. Every manager must have the ability to communicate, motivate, and inspire. While not all managers-leaders have the same combination of skills, the goal is to develop and integrate to the greatest extent possible the qualities of leadership in management.

In recent times, examples abound of leaders and managers failing in their basic responsibilities to their organizations and to society. Corporate giants Worldcom and Arthur Andersen, among others, collapsed because of ethical and professional lapses in the senior leadership. The destruction of records, a hallmark in almost all these cases, not only destroyed the integrity of the business record, but undermined the very foundations of the organizations involved and led directly to great public disillusionment and mistrust. The archival manager, regardless of institutional setting, contributes to the health of the organization and the wider society by exercising leadership in developing and maintaining an archival and records management program grounded in law, regulation, and the fundamental principles of the profession.

Suggested Readings

James MacGregor Burns, *Leadership* (New York: Harper-Collins Publishers, 1995), provides informative insights into the nature and role of leadership. *Harvard Business Review* has numerous articles on varied aspects of leadership, including those by Henry Mintzberg and Abraham Zaleznik, which are listed in the footnotes.

Recommendations for understanding behavior and its impact in the workplace include Daniel Goleman, *Working with Emotional Intelligence* (New York: Bantam Books, 1998); and Otto Kroeger and Janet M. Thuesen, *Type Talk at Work* (New York: Dell Publishing, 1992).

Several library journals, such as *Library Administration and Management, Library Administration,* and *Library Trends,* contain excellent articles on leadership issues. Significant articles include Sue R. Faerman, "Organizational Change and Leadership Style," *Journal of Library Administration* 19, nos. 3–4 (1996): 55–79; Michael T. Sweeney, "Leadership in the Post-Hierarchical Library," *Library Trends* 43 (Summer 1994): 62–94; and Merrily E. Taylor, "Getting It All Together: Leadership Requirements for the Future of Information Services," *Journal of Library Administration* 20 (1995): 9–24.

Chapter 3

Organizational Complexity: A New Management Paradigm

We are all familiar with the ancient Chinese proverb "May you live in interesting times." Depending on one's point of view, this can be a blessing or a curse. Managers today, including archival managers, are living through some interesting times indeed. It is not enough to master the functions and skills discussed in the first two chapters of this manual. It is also necessary to understand the profound changes affecting contemporary society and how institutions and management must adapt. This chapter focuses on the complexity of contemporary organizations and how managing often complicated institutional relationships has transformed the roles and responsibilities of those leading archival programs.

Change Factors

The most difficult challenge of all—managing change—is also among the most important but least understood aspects of the modern manager's portfolio. Obviously, organizations are not self-contained; they face a variety of external and internal factors resulting at times in dramatic change. Larger institutions often have organizational development specialists who assist managers in identifying factors stimulating change and in developing strategies to manage change. Most medium and small archives may not have access to such expertise. But a manager

Archives need to keep informed of new technology as well as maintain older technology to support collections. Austin History Center, Austin Public Library

should anticipate major change factors and should work with colleagues in creating successful opportunities for navigating change.

Information technology is a major change factor. This will be discussed in greater detail in chapter 7. It is enough here to note that the information revolution has transformed internal work processes, such as archival description, while immeasurably enhancing access to finding aids and holdings through the Internet. Among other things, service expectations have risen because of automation, straining often limited staff resources. From the institutional perspective, other issues arise. What actions taken or planned by the archives' parent organization will change the way it creates records? What steps must be taken to enable the archives to receive, preserve, and make accessible these records?

Demographic and social factors also affect archival organizations as well as all other segments of society. An aging population, for example, has more leisure time to pursue family and community history. Single-parent families and those where both spouses work are facing changes in child care, family and parental leave, flexible work hours, and telecommuting. These factors affect how work is organized and managed. (See figure 3-1.)

Legal and regulatory factors force organizational change on an ongoing basis. Over time, most archivists (and archival managers) become familiar with issues related to copyright law, deeds of gift, tax law relevant to acquisitions, records law, and privacy legislation.

Figure 3-1 Demographic and Social Factors

Changes	Possible Effects
1. Aging American population	1. Increased leisure time 2. Increased demand for service records 3. Increased genealogical interest
2. Increase in single parent heads of households	1. Demand for child-care services at work 2. Flexible work hours 3. Ability to perform work at home
3. Increasingly diverse multicultural society	1. Development of nontraditional hiring and promotional strategies 2. Revised recruitment strategies for archival education programs 3. Changes in how managers communicate and evaluate employees

But, archival managers must also be cognizant of developments affecting the climate in which their institutions must operate. Changes in laws governing personnel (fair labor practices, occupational health and safety codes, equal employment opportunity), facilities (building codes, zoning, historic site preservation), and finance (a varied set of requirements depending on whether one manages a private, local, state, corporate, or federal archival operation) must all be considered.

Changing Roles

The industrial era, which began in the nineteenth century and continued well into the twentieth, saw the development and expansion of large, bureaucratic organizational structures in industry, labor, government, and religious denominations. Max Weber, the noted sociologist of the early twentieth century, documented the nature and operational traits of bureaucratic organizations.[1] During the twentieth century, most archives developed within larger bureaucracies and mimicked the structure and behavior of the parent organization.

These institutions were, and in many cases still are, typically managed in a top-down command-and-control hierarchical structure. Typical of the industrial era model, they are built around division of labor, span of control, and sharply defined functional departments or units. The management basically makes all the decisions, with lower levels of management tasked to implement the decisions. Front-line or operational staff carry out orders and send information up the chain of command. As previously discussed, this model has the virtues of stability and consistency, but has its distinct limitations, particularly from the perspective of adapting to change.

In the United States, the period since the 1960s has been marked not only by political and social ferment but also by profound changes in the workplace. Foreign business competition and other factors forced industry and labor to focus on quality, simplify work processes, and streamline organizational structures. First-line workers and staff came to be seen as key factors for success rather than as widgets to be managed. At the same time, the American workforce in general has become more diverse, educated, and desirous of autonomy. The re-engineering or re-invention drive has profoundly affected the corporate and industrial sectors and is now moving into the public and nonprofit sectors.

A major change engine has been the telecommunications revolution. The industrial economy's turn into a service economy, and

1 G. Edward Evans, Patricia Layzell Ward, and Bendik Rugaas, *Management Basics for Information Professionals* (New York and London: Neal-Schuman Publishers, Inc., 2000), 49–52.

information services in particular, has helped transform how we live and work. Whether we are considering fax messaging, cellular phones, or computer networks, direct communications eliminate the middle-person and the middle manager, resulting in streamlined, simpler, and more efficient work processes. Electronic mail is perhaps one of the most democratizing forces in modern history. The traditional chain of command, where direction moves downward and information moves upward, is rendered increasingly irrelevant as information can move horizontally and vertically throughout an organization with little or no control.

The pressure for effectiveness, efficiency, and the bottom line is felt in the public and nonprofit sectors as well as in the private sector. Consumers used to shopping on-line twenty-four hours a day and "surfing the net" for information cannot understand or accept slow, paper-based processes and procedures—hallmarks of the traditional bureaucracy. Public libraries, to take one example, are transforming themselves into information service providers with automated patron services and internal work processes. The emphasis is on speed, rapid turnaround, and quality. Archives, wherever located, are under similar pressures and expectations.

Organizational Complexity: The New Paradigm

This ongoing workplace revolution is also transforming the role of managers. The functions identified by Fayol and modified by his successors remain required in the workplace. Leadership in management continues as essential for organizational success. Yet, how these functions are carried out is undergoing great change. Information technology has revolutionized communications within organizations and between organizations and the external environment. Managers are no longer commanding or directing staff (á la Fayol), passing decisions down and information up the hierarchical ladder. Rather, in a world increasingly based on the effective acquisition and utilization of knowledge swiftly absorbed and communicated, the new paradigm for managers is one of complex organizational relationships. Picture a web of relationships connecting the manager with staff, other parts

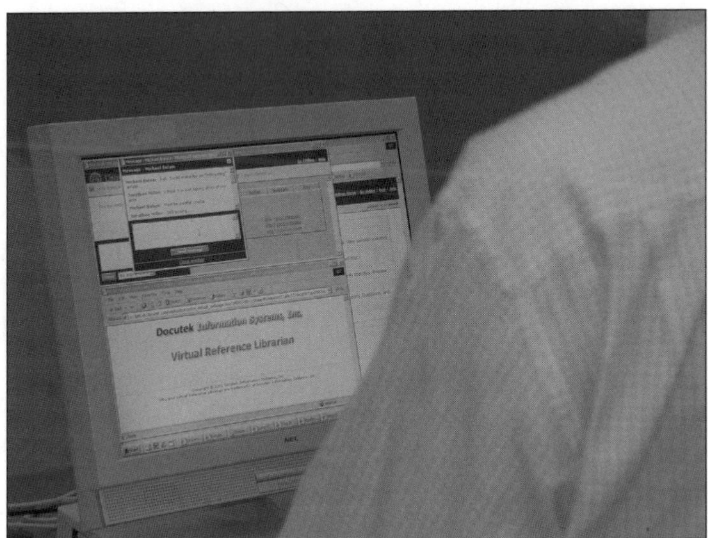

Technological advances may place demands on archives to provide service in new ways, such as through chat reference sessions, to support increased collection use by researchers that aren't necessarily local. Photo by Gregory McCormmick, University Library System, University of Pittsburgh

of the parent institution, and numerous groups external to the organization. Successful management is based on understanding the complicated and changeable nature of organizational relationships and developing relationships to further the archival mission.

Particularly in any organization that is totally knowledge based, such as archives, manuscript repositories, and libraries, managers cannot operate self-contained units. The varying ways in which managers relate to staff, to other parts of the institution, and to the complex world of customers (i.e., patrons, researchers), constituent groups, and the general public demand a new set of skills. The ability to manage diverse relationships is the ultimate measure of a manager's success.

Building Internal Relationships

The archival organization operates increasingly within the re-engineered and automated workplace. No longer can managers just assign and monitor work, report to supervisors, and operate in traditional ways. The flood of information coming in via the Internet, the Web, and the intranet is transforming the work environment. Staff members are able to communicate and perform their jobs in this automated milieu across the organization, the city, the state, the nation, and the world. Whether it is formally recognized or not, staff members are not really constrained to operate and communicate within traditional, hierarchical channels.

In fact, modern management theory, whether expressed in total quality management, business process re-engineering, or knowledge management, emphasizes the critical importance of staff empowerment and investment in the institution's mission if long-term success is to be achieved. Corporate restructuring and tight budgets at all levels of government place archival organizations and staff members in potential peril. The archives must contribute to the corporation's bottom line and its effectiveness. In the governmental, nonprofit, and educational arenas, the archives must be viewed clearly as critical for success.

The manager's principle contribution to achieving success for the organization is in managing multiple relationships. The archival and program staff must be "managed" in new ways. More and more, the manager assumes the role of coach and mentor. The educated, Internet-savvy, and mobile workplace of today requires leaders who assist staff in developing individually and as a group. Teamwork, whether formal, ad-hoc, or both, dominates the workplace. The manager as coach must aid the staff in gaining the skills and the autonomy needed to make decisions about the work at hand.

The coach's job is to facilitate staff interaction and cooperation, obtaining any training needed to enhance individual or group skills. The information-age manager has to aid staff members in learning decision-making and consensus-building skills so that they can make as many work-process-related decisions as possible. This empowerment of staff, whether it takes place on the factory floor or the archives' processing room, reflects the widespread technological and social changes that have dominated over the past fifty years. This new relationship with the staff views as shared tasks previously considered solely the prerogative of management. The manager in the roles of leader and coach shares responsibility and authority with those directly involved in a particular work process or project. This shared approach can take place in a variety of guises grouped under the term "teamwork." Teams and how they work will be discussed in more detail in subsequent chapters. Generally, teams range from those tasked with ad-hoc special projects to those working on recurring processes such as accessioning, processing, or reference service. Teams, to a greater or lesser extent, participate in such management responsibilities as planning, assigning work, and performance evaluation. This is not an abdication on the part of management. The relationship of shared responsibility with the staff is vital for the unit to perform at full effectiveness. Anything less could ultimately spell doom for the organization.

The successful manager, however, must relate with the staff as more than a coach. Organizations can seem fragmented to staff as they and their functions undergo re-engineering, restructuring, and outsourcing. The manager must become a builder, helping both staff within the unit and other colleagues to communicate and share their expertise and creativity. Unrelated to formal structure or teams, this is a delicate task, for a manager's heavy hand can squelch staff initiative. But the manager's encouragement of communities of practice (discussed in chapter 1), for example, can stimulate the sharing of knowledge and aid in resolution of technical and professional issues. The manager's support in assisting these groups with time, space (where appropriate), and technology can substantially contribute to organizational transformation.

Another tool to help the manager build an effective relationship with staff is known as "hot groups." Neither a team nor a formal or structured unit, a hot group is "a task-obsessed state of mind, an attitude shared by a group's members."[2] This phenomenon began in the IT world of Silicon Valley and has spread to a variety of other organizations. One good example cited in management literature is the coalescing of a group of naval and civilian employees who banded together to overhaul a U.S. Navy vessel into a guided missile cruiser in

2 Jean Lipman-Bluman and Harold J. Leavitt, *Hot Groups: Seeding Them, Feeding Them, and Using Them to Ignite Your Organization* (New York and Oxford: Oxford University Press, 1999), XXIII, 3–28.

an unbelievable twelve-month timeframe. A hot group feels itself totally committed to completing a vital, seemingly unachievable task. This is a relatively short-lived experience during which everything is subordinated to the task.

This nearly spontaneous coming together has several requirements. A dynamic leader needs to emerge, such as the rather junior naval officer in the guided missile cruiser case. Upper-level managers need to support the group as it comes together and takes over the project. Rules, regulations, and bureaucratic routines must fall by the wayside, and the senior manager needs to ensure that this happens. Certain situations can arise in the archival unit or the parent organization where such total, task-obsessive commitment is crucial to achieve what is a vital but seemingly impossible task. We are not talking about routine operations. As builder and nurturer, the manager must be sensitive as a group begins to form around a task it views as critical, and then he or she must help eliminate organizational roadblocks. When the task is completed, the group disbands.

The point in discussing teams, communities of practice, and hot groups is to emphasize the need for the manager to be open-minded, alert to situations and possibilities, and perceptive about the essential nature of relationship building as the key to managerial and organizational success. The archival manager may never be involved with communities of practice or hot groups. But every archival manager will have to learn how to operate effectively in collaborative models of one sort or another.

Building External Relationships

The manager must also build and sustain relationships beyond the unit and the projects and operations of the unit. In reality, the manager's full-time job is networking or relationship building. Managers operate in a competitive, cost-conscious, and technologically driven organizational climate. In a number of settings, such as universities, corporations, and the public sector, other parts of an organization can compete with the archives as the provider of information and even of records. Building relationships with other parts of the institution and with constituent groups outside the institution is extremely important. The manager (and the entire staff as well) must market the archives for its value, service, and contribution to the bottom line.

Whether the archives is part of a corporation, a religious denomination, a union, a university, or a government, the demands for quality work and service and competitive efficiency are relentless. Even in the public sector, programs that are seen as ineffective, too expensive, or irrelevant will disappear, most likely through consolidation and reorganization, and never to the benefit of the organization. Periodic economic recessions have a severe impact on government revenues, and archival programs often feel the brunt. If archival managers have not built sustainable relationships with other parts of the parent institution and with customers, donors, and appropriators outside the institution, trouble can be expected. Building such relationships requires skills in communications, public relations, marketing, and sales. These skills were probably not part of most archival managers' education or professional development, but they are fundamental tools for relationship building and must be developed. (See relevant chapters of this manual for further discussion.)

A basic mindset for external relationship building is the concept of partnership. Forming partnerships with corporations, relevant constituent groups, or other organizations with compatible missions, services, or holdings can aid in meeting the archival program's objectives. Such partnerships aid in exploiting opportunities and coping with threats. These partnerships can result in the sharing of skills and expertise, information, joint projects, and mutual support. They require the archival manager to reach out to the external environment using the communication tools of negotiation and persuasion.

Conclusion

The most successful managers are those who ask themselves every day, "What are the opportunities for partnerships and building relationships, and whom should I contact?" Figuring out how to contribute to other units and organizations and forming mutually beneficial relationships can help the archives survive turbulent organizational times. The manager must constantly demonstrate that the archives is so valuable, so needed for organizational success, that the archives not only survives but grows. Organizations (like individuals) either move forward or decline. The status quo is never truly maintained. The manager's major responsibility is to see that the archives moves forward. Management is not an additional duty or a step up the organizational ladder. It is a calling with rewards for success and penalties for failure. Unfortunately, when the manager fails, the program also suffers, as do staff and patrons. A step-by-step look at the actual tasks that confront managers follows, along with suggestions and resources available for the archival manager seeking to succeed in a new and complex environment.

Suggested Readings

The ongoing changes in the way work processes and organizations are understood and managed are reflected in management literature. Some of the most significant works include Michael Hammer and James Champy, *Reengineering the Corporation* (New York: Harper Business, 1993); and James Champy, *Reengineering Management* (New York: Harper-Collins Publishers, 1995), both of which challenge traditional, hierarchical, and compartmentalized methods of work. Rafael Aguayo, *Dr. Deming: The American Who Taught the Japanese About Quality* (New York: Simon and Schuster, 1990), uses biography to describe the impact of the quality movement on American industry and its methods of understanding work, the worker, and the customer.

G. Edward Evans, et al., *Management Basics for Information Professionals* (New York: Neal-Schuman Publishers, 2000), provides an extensive list of sources and further reading for dealing with changes in library services over time. Though not directly related to archives, the sources provide rich material for archival managers seeking more depth and perspective. Helpful works in the area of teaming include Ann Harper and Bob Harper, *Team Barriers: Actions for Overcoming the Blocks to Empowerment, Involvement, and High Performance* (New York: M.W. Corporation, 1994); and Carl Harshman and Steven Phillips, *Teaming Up: Achieving Organizational Transformation* (San Diego: Pfeiffer and Company), 1994.

Chapter 4

Foundations of Organizational Success

The previous chapter explored the new paradigm of organizational complexity and a relationship-based work environment as the core of the manager's focus, tasks, and accomplishments. The same technological and social changes that have transformed the work of managers have similarly affected how organizations develop, function, and relate to other entities. The concept of organizational relationships reflects new realities in organizational theory, increasing awareness of the importance of organizational culture, and the impact of the quality movement and knowledge management. It is the key to organizational success.

New Realities

Various organizational theories articulated and developed in the past several decades have moved far beyond Frederick W. Taylor's "scientific" approach, which viewed work and the organization from a "machine" perspective by emphasizing the division of work into specialized tasks or functions with a command-and-control management structure. Concepts such as group behavior, group dynamics, and collaborative work processes developed by Mary Parker Follett and the Human Relations School in the first half of the twentieth century have found their way into contemporary organizational theory.

Contingency theory, for example, sees organizational design as based on the nature of the work performed and the broader environmental climate in other parts of the organization or outside of it. From the *quality movement* perspective, the environment for the organization is set by the demands of customers. In an archives, customers may demand that the holdings be described and in an on-line catalog; that archival records be available for research via the Internet; or that on-line ordering be made available. All this is based on customer expectations of quality and service. Organizational structure would depend on the demands made for information and services.

Resource dependence theory focuses on the interdependence of the organization with other entities in its environment. This includes relationships with organizations that provide records to the archives; relationships between the archives and other entities that provide information or services; and even relationships with records and knowledge competitors such as in the university setting, libraries, academic departments, or even the intranet. Other theories also involve relationships. *Institutional theory* studies how organizations are affected by their institutional environment, particularly culture and value systems. *Organizational learning* explores how and why organizations change their capabilities and how learning changes routines and practices.

Integral to all these theories is an appreciation of organizational culture. This is difficult to define and in great measure difficult to change. Organizational structures and relationships are deeply rooted in the culture of the group. In fact, multiple cultures may exist within an organization or perhaps even within the archives itself. This may be due to functional alignments or geographical dispersion. Shared values and norms for group behavior evolve over time as managers and staff interact and develop strategies for successfully performing tasks and resolving problems and challenges as they arise. Cultures can be strong or weak. How well organizations respond to crises or turnover in leaders or key staff, for example, indicates the adaptability or rigidity of the culture. Little about any organization's culture is clearly documented, but it is contained in everything from the strategic plan to organizational effectiveness to stories told around the water cooler or the lunch table. The prudent manager realizes that it takes time to understand an organization's culture. The manager must come to appreciate how leadership is exercised and by whom, how the organization handles routine and extraordinary demands, and how the organization values staff and customers.

Managing knowledge and organizational learning are key tasks for the contemporary manager and are at the heart of organizational relationships. As mentioned in chapter 1, knowledge management is emerging in both theory and practice. Yet broadly stated, learning in organizations is "a collective sensemaking process that follows an identifiable progression of cognitive activities. This progression begins with individuals' noticing events of potential significance for the organization (data)" and then moving through an interpretive framework leading to individual, group, and organizational knowledge.[1]

Figure 4-1 represents five learning cycles and is not meant to be understood as an organizational chart but rather to convey that knowledge exists in individuals, work groups, and the overall organization. The manager needs to be aware of this in developing and sustaining organizational relationships. In nurturing organizational competence, the manager must understand how staff members interpret data and information and how they turn them into knowledge. To do this, the manager must consider formal and informal relationships such as teams, communities of practice, and hot groups for learning, competence, and ultimately enhanced quality and productivity. There are organizational relationships within the unit, to other parts of the institution, and to the external environment of customers, records creators, donors, and supporters.

Organizational relationships are complex, much like the web of relationships the manager must build and sustain. But amid complexity there also must be clarity when it comes to the archives' authority, purpose, placement, and performance. A foundation in clarity helps the manager to successfully pursue new opportunities and relationships in the complex world of knowledge with a clear mind.

---

1 Ron Sanchez, ed., *Knowledge Management and Organizational Competence* (New York: Oxford University Press, 2001), 4–5.

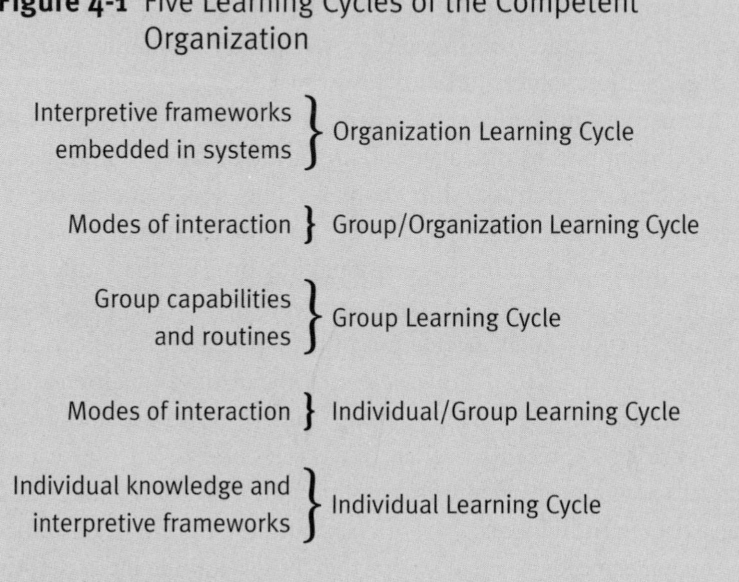

Figure 4-1 Five Learning Cycles of the Competent Organization

(Courtesy of Oxford University Press, found in Ron Sanchez, Knowledge Management and Organizational Competence, *2001, p. 8)*

Authority and Purpose

Because they are responsible for processing the records of their parent institutions, all archives are part of larger structures. Manuscript repositories may be independent in theory, but most are part of libraries or historical societies. As part of a larger agency, an archives has a specific mission, responsibility, and authority. If the archives is a governmental agency, its functions are usually dictated by government statute or regulation. Corporate and religious archives often have their activities outlined in bylaws, constitutions, or institutional policies. A university archives may have its activities governed by the board of trustees or at the discretion of the president or provost.

Whatever the type of archives, it is the responsibility of the archival manager to develop a formal statement that outlines its mission, responsibility, and authority in relation to its parent institution. This overall policy statement should clearly state the mission of the

Processing photographic collections at the Center for Creative Photography. CENTER FOR CREATIVE PHOTOGRAPHY.

archives; what it collects, preserves, and makes available; the audience that the archives serves; and, at least in a broad, overarching manner, the measurements for a successful program. The policy statement should also address the issue of the disposition of archival records in the event the archives or parent institution should cease to exist. Finally, the statement should delineate the system of accountability for any specialized programs such as records management. (See figure 4-2.) This policy document must be authorized by the institution's highest administrative body. Such authority allows archivists to carry out their responsibilities without questions being raised about the support of the parent agency. The policy statement is part of the formal process to establish and clarify organizational relationships. However, remaining limited to only the relationships laid out in the statement will not alone ensure organizational success. Other forms of organizational relationships crucial for success are covered later in this chapter.

Figure 4-2 Policy Statement

1. Value of a Policy Statement
   A. Creates a public statement of archival purpose.
   B. Defines a collecting policy.
   C. Defines an access policy.
   D. Outlines the parameters of the archivist's responsibility and authority.
2. Outlines of a Policy Statement
   A. Legal authority
   The statement must begin by indicating the name of the repository and the name of the parent institution; it should outline the archives' legal authority to collect, preserve, and make available its records. Such a statement should prohibit the removal of material from the archives without the archivist's approval as well as outline what should happen to the collection in the event that the archival program is dissolved or disbanded.
   B. Purpose
   The archives must have a mission statement defining archival duties and tasks. (See chapter 5 on planning.)
   C. Position and authority of the archivist
   The statement should outline the archivist's role within the archives as well as the relationship with the parent institution or governing board. It should detail the archivist's legal authority to carry out archival tasks and may indicate general qualifications for the archivist and a method of selecting appropriate personnel.
   D. Outline of responsibilities
   The policy statement should outline specific duties for the archivist and archival staff. This should indicate appropriate relationships between the archives and the parent institution, the archives and an advisory committee (if one exists), the archives and donors, and the archives and researchers.
   E. Collecting policy
   This should indicate why the archives exists and what type of material is collected. (This may be supplemented by a separate and more detailed collecting policy.)

(continued)

Figure 4-2 continued

F. Access policy
There should be a general statement outlining who may use the archives collection and under what conditions. (This may be supplemented by a separate and more detailed access policy.)

G. Records management
If the archives is responsible for records management, this role should be carefully delineated.

H. Definitions
The statement should clarify archival responsibility by defining such archival terms as archives, records, access, and appraisal in the policy statement.

(Concept courtesy of the Society of California Archivists)

Organizational Placement

One of the most important issues for any archives is its placement in the institution's organizational structure. The archives' position in the larger organizational structure can either enhance or hinder it in carrying out its mission. In addition, the archival manager must have a clear understanding of the lines of communication and authority and be able to develop strong and supportive working relationships with supervisors and managers in other parts of the parent institution. The archives' placement will vary depending upon the type of parent institution and its mission. Placement can have a major impact on an archives' program, impinging on such issues as

- The ability of the archives to carry out its mission;
- The level of financial and program support for the archives; and
- The commonality of purpose between the archives and the department that supervises its activities.

There is no one perfect solution, and placements vary even among comparable types of institutions. (See figures 4-3 and 4-4.)

Figure 4-3 Placement in the Institution's Organizational Structure

State Archives: Secretary of State, State Library, Department of Administrative Services, State Historical Society.

University Archives: University President or Provost, Library, Public Relations, University Secretary or Registrar.

Institutional or Corporate Archives: Corporate Secretary, Public Relations, Library, Legal Affairs, Management Information Systems.

Figure 4-4 A Comparison of the Positive and Negative Aspects of Placing a University Archives under the University Library as Opposed to the President's Office

President's Office

Positive features:

1. The president's office has authority over the entire university campus and can mandate the transfer of records or the development of records retention schedules.
2. The president has greater discretion in budgeting funds and staff needed to carry out an archival program.

Negative features:

1. The president's office seldom deals with either information management or the tools needed to carry out such functions.
2. The training and institutional outlook of the president's staff is dissimilar to those of the archives' staff. While understanding the administrative value of preserving records, the president's staff may fail to see the importance of making material available; it may even oppose access by researchers.

(continued)

Figure 4-4 continued

University Library

Positive features:

1. Both archives and libraries deal with information packaged in various forms.
2. Libraries have bibliographic networks that may be used by the archives to describe its collection.
3. Librarians and archivists usually have similar training and are committed to making materials available for use.

Negative features:

1. In a library setting, an archives may be several administrative levels from the top library official, who is in turn several levels below the rank of the senior university administrator. Such distance can make it difficult to obtain support and cooperation for a university-wide archival program.
2. An archives is one function within a library and may fail to receive an adequate budget or support staff.
3. Because library administrators may not understand archives, they may not support a strong, separate archival program.

Given a choice, what type of placement should an archival manager seek? First, a manager should attempt to locate the archives as close to the top of the administrative chain as possible. For example, archival managers are generally able to generate much greater support and cooperation if they report to the library director rather than to the assistant head of the special collections department. Second, the archives should establish a separate identity. The archives must have a separate budget line, an annual report requirement, and a prominent position on the parent institution's Web site or intranet, and it must utilize any other tool that will allow greater independence or institutional stature. Third, the archives should seek placement under a department with a strong interest in archives that can give it adequate support. Fourth, the archives should seek placement in a department that has a successful record of accomplishment.

Over time, situations arise that require the placement of the archives to be re-evaluated. This can occur when the archives is still a relatively new program without entrenched interests vested in continuing its current placement or during a major reorganization of the parent institution. Regardless of the circumstances, the archival manager needs to cultivate high-level support and build strong relationships with other organizational managers. In certain situations, obtaining the services of a consultant or outside review committee can lay the foundation for change. For example, an archival collection in the library of a religious denomination may be an overlooked resource and an undervalued asset. An archival expert, preferably with standing in the field of religious archives or the denomination (optimum!) can identify issues of placement, program, and financial support to assist the library director in understanding that the collection is an important knowledge asset for the institution which can help to build relationships beyond the institution. Also, the expert can lay out space needs; processing, preservation, and reference requirements; and resource needs (i.e., equipment, supplies, staff) for a multiyear period.

The placement of the archives within its parent organization is the basic foundation for all archival programs. The ability of an archives to achieve its goals is directly related to the resources that are provided by the institution, and placement can be all-important in gaining or retaining needed resources. Strong support will not always lead to an outstanding archival program if there is poor leadership, but the lack of support will inevitably lead to failure, even under the best archival manager.

Organizing Work

Increasingly, work in all organizations, including archives, is being performed across functions, disciplines, and organizational boundaries. Teams are increasingly used to accomplish work and achieve organizational objectives. Jon R. Katzenbach and Douglas K. Smith provide a good working definition: "A team is a small number of people with complementary skills who are committed to a common purpose, performance goals, and a particular approach for which they hold themselves mutually accountable."[2] Teamwork is not a recent phenomenon. But as organizations in the public and private sectors increasingly reduce bureaucratic layers, and emphasize quality and customer service, alternatives to the top-down command-and-control, hierarchical structure are coming to the fore.

Any form of organizational structure, including teaming, must flow from work processes. Work drives structure. Analysis of work processes, done by flow charting and systems analysis among other techniques, is the first essential step in developing an internal organizational structure. (See figure 4-5.) Work products, quality requirements, turn-around times, and other desired outcomes must be identified along with any structural impediments to success.

In addition to ongoing work involving functional tasks, such as processing, preservation, and reference service, projects, special assignments, and strategic initiatives require a group effort. There are a variety of types of teams. (See figure 4-6.) These can consist of the ongoing category, including policy-making management teams, work process teams (functional or cross-functional), and quality circles focused on improving work processes. In some situations, ongoing teams can become self-directed, fully responsible for all aspects of personnel, budget, and work performance. Examples of time-limited teams include task forces, project teams, and committees. The scope and long-term impact of the work, the roles and responsibilities of the team, and the skills, knowledge, and competence required by management and team members determine the type of team or collaborative work group utilized.

Even in traditional structures (see figure 4-7), work is often performed across unit lines with temporary or informal teams, which may not appear on the organizational chart. The transition from a top-down structure to a collaborative, team-based structure is difficult. Not all teams are successful. In the corporate sector, change results from economic competition and continuous mergers and downsizing. In the public and nonprofit sectors, the continued competition for scarce resources and the consequent need for high-performance quality, success, and recognition drive the forces of change.

---

2 Jon R. Katzenbach and Doublas K. Smith, "The Discipline of Teams," *Harvard Business Review* (March–April 1993): 111–20.

Figure 4-5 Flowchart Showing Process for Review and Approval of Retention and Disposition Schedules at Delaware Public Archives

Retention Schedule is submitted or prepared

Do the records have any characteristics of long-term value?

No

Yes

Get feedback/ input from appropriate staff

"No brainer" appraisals

Final Schedule to State Archivist for Approval

Full analysis/ appraisal

Records still display archival qualities

No

Yes

Schedule completed

Prepare appraisal report

Review by committee and change by analyst

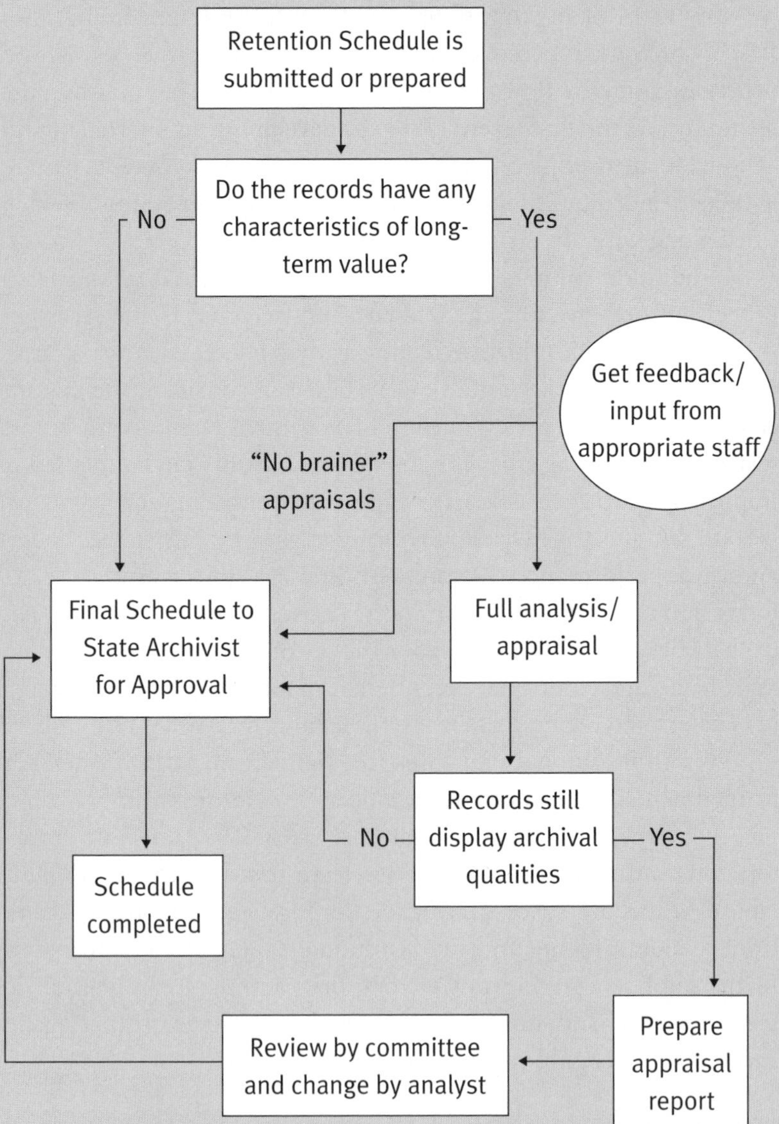

(Concept courtesy of the Delaware Public Archives)

Figure 4-6 Types of Teams

Ongoing	Limited (by time, assignment, or function)
1. Management teams (Policy making)	1. Task forces
2. Work process teams (Functional or cross-functional)	2. Project teams
3. Quality circles	3. Committees

Figure 4-7

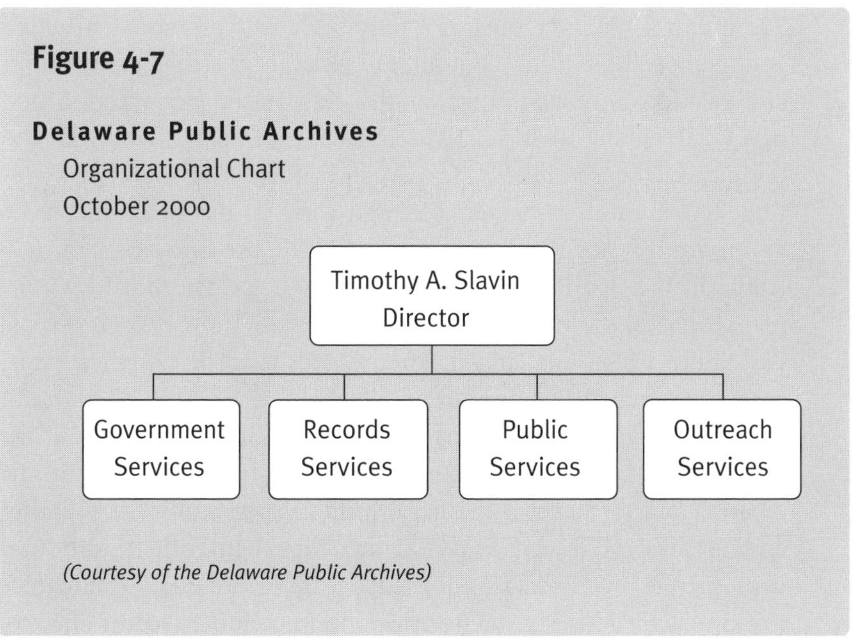

(Courtesy of the Delaware Public Archives)

If the archives' unit has two or more employees or volunteers, then a collaborative work approach is more effective and efficient. Two archivists can process a collection better than one doing every step alone in a linear or sequential fashion. Whether working on ad-hoc task forces, committees, and teams of experts, or with ongoing work process teams, archival staff will need support from the parent institution in the areas of group dynamics, communications, compensation, group decision making, and systems thinking. (See chapter 8 for further discussion on team competencies.) The team approach is difficult because society is accustomed to living and working in hierarchical structures. But a flexible, creative, and responsive internal organizational structure designed to produce high performance is as critical for the archives' success as good placement in the overall organization.

Relationships and Partners

The archival manager must not only build organizational structure and relationships within the unit, but must forge strong partnerships and relationships with units in the rest of the organization and beyond. In many ways, archives are living in both a custodial and postcustodial environment. Textual and audiovisual collections continue to exist and, in fact, are often growing. At the same time, more and more records in the parent organization are being created electronically in a distributed environment. As the postcustodial environment comes to the fore over time, archivists must move beyond storing, describing, preserving, and making records available. Archival managers must view the organization's records as a resource and source of knowledge. The manager must work with colleagues throughout the organization in enterprisewide learning. This involves records in the archives and throughout the organization. Specifically, the manager and archival staff can form partnerships with other units and demonstrate how to create knowledge from records. This can involve working with others in the organization to conduct records analyses that include both analyzing records systems and interviewing records creators and users to understand what transpires informally in the knowledge-gaining process.

When archival managers and staff understand how learning occurs, they can work with IT specialists and other specialists in supporting communities of practice and hot groups. The archival manager can only participate in these organizationwide experiences if he or she moves beyond the custodial mindset.

Information is critical for decision making. If the archival manager can foster a mindset focused on outcomes rather than outputs (i.e., inventories, guides, finding aids), then it becomes possible to forge relationships beyond the unit. For example, partnerships with units creating electronic records might include a shared responsibility for records. Also, archival managers and staff can get involved in the design and implementation of recordkeeping systems. This would provide support to ensure authentic and reliable records and to the knowledge needs of the organization.

Archivists need to meet and work with other information professionals such as librarians, records managers, and IT specialists. Why not identify specific issues or problems in the organization and seek to form a community of practice with other information professionals and program managers? Through the Internet and Web this can be opened up outside the organization. Once again, it is important to stress that archival managers and staff must emerge from their units and mix it up with the learning and knowledge needs of the organization. This will mean going to seminars and workshops on knowledge management, information technology, electronic records, and organizational theory to understand what is really happening in the workplace. Identify workshops offered by professional associations such as the Society of American Archivists, ARMA International, National Association of Government Archives and Records Administrators, and regional groups, and then participate with a clear goal of what needs to be learned to function as an effective partner.

In forging relationships beyond the unit, the archival manager must develop an effective working relationship with those in the parent institution with administrative responsibility for the archives program. This can be a superior or a governing board. A governing board, in contrast to an advisory committee, usually has authority to approve or disapprove policies and procedures recommended by the archival manager. Its recommendations may be final, or it may be only an intermediary whose recommendations need the approval of some higher authority.

Good internal communication is one of the most critical factors in building effective reporting relationships with the parent institution. The archival manager must make a continued effort to inform the governing authority of all major aspects of the archival program. Such communication can take a number of forms. The periodic written report, whether weekly, monthly, or quarterly, should describe the full range of archival objectives, highlight achievements and problems, and note any trends that may affect the archives or the parent institution. The archival manager should ensure that the archival program is featured in any formal annual report. Also, the archives should either put out its own staff newsletter or ensure that the program participates in any internal publication produced by the parent institution. For even wider internal dissemination and attention, archival services and program activities should be listed on the intranet so that all parts of the parent organization will be aware of the archival program.

The archival manager should also make sure that the archival staff participates in those institutional committees, task forces, and working groups whose tasks directly or indirectly affect the archival program. This will enable institutional leaders to recognize and value the skills and expertise that archivists contribute to the organization. Another important reporting relationship involves the budget. The archival manager must ensure that the archives has a line item in the budget and that the manager is involved in all aspects of the budget process, from formulation through execution. The archival manager must, on a regular basis throughout the fiscal year, communicate to the parent institution or any governing authority unexpected needs that have arisen or, if budget cuts are contemplated, their impact on the mission of the archives and the parent institution.

Creating and sustaining partnerships and relationships for the archival program within the organization are clearly critical necessities. Just as significant for many archival programs is the support received from related, external groups.

Support Organizations

Support organizations can serve as both buffers and advocates for the archives' cause. One such organization is the advisory committee, normally established to advise the archival manager. Such committees, usually appointed by the parent organization, can be drawn from the institutional hierarchy, research community, donors, or constituent groups. Depending upon the type of institution, the advisory committee has the potential to serve the archives' program both as an advocate and as a communication network, bringing information to the archival manager and disseminating information to other members of the parent body. Advisory committees should provide advice and communication if they are to have any value. To prevent organizational confusion, the advisory committee should not be involved in operational control or oversight.

Advisory committees are particularly helpful when an archival program is just beginning or when a new archival manager has come on the job. In any event, if the members are carefully selected, the committee can represent a variety of constituencies important to the archival program. They can speak for the archives to resource allocators, provide specialized knowledge and expertise, and serve as informal publicists for the archives' cause. The archival manager needs to be closely involved, if not the determining voice, in who is selected and how the process of selection is carried out.

Another type of support organization is a "friends of the archives" group or a foundation that can assist with publicity and financial support. To be fully effective as a fund-raising support arm, the friends group or the foundation would need to be incorporated under provisions of the Internal Revenue Code (Section 501) so that tax-exempt contributions could be made to support the archives. These groups generally operate under a constitution and bylaws with an elected board and officers. Made up of donors, researchers, and other interested supporters, they expand the number of people actively involved in the work of the archives. Friends groups can be useful support organizations, while not interfering with the archival manager's ability to control the archives' internal operation. They can provide introductions to sources of outside funding, host receptions for archival exhibitions, support scholarly programs, print publications, or reproduce important documents for sale or gifts.

Conclusion

Creating effective organizational relationships is one of the major contributions that a manager can make to the archival program. It takes time and experience for a manager to understand an organization's culture, its knowledge needs, and how to structure work processes and staff to meet the operational imperatives of the archives and the wider strategic needs of the organization. In addition to time and experience, the manager must stay intelligently and professionally alert with continued education and training. Seminars and workshops that deal with organizational development and change management, for example, can aid the manager in obtaining new insights, perspective, and understanding—all vital in an era of organizational complexity.

Suggested Readings

While material on organizational development and relationships in archival literature is limited, a good reference tool is Gregory S. Hunter, *Developing and Maintaining Practical Archives: A How-To-Do-It Manual* (New York and London: Neal-Schuman Publishers, Inc., 1996). From a related field, G. Edward Evans, et al., *Management Basics for Information Professionals,* discusses organizational development from the wider perspective of internal and external organizational environments. John P. Kotter and James L. Heskott, *Corporate Culture and Performance* (New York: The Free Press, 1992), explores the multiple levels of organizational culture, how they are perpetuated, and how they affect the organization for good or ill. This is an easy-to-read and interesting text. Robert E. Cole and W. Richard Scott edited a series of essays on *The Quality Movement and Organizational Theory* (Thousand Oaks, Calif.: Sage Publications, Inc., 2000). The introduction by the editors is a brief but illuminating review of various organizational theories, and it lays the groundwork for understanding how the quality movement emphasis on external customers has changed organizational environments.

Other useful works on new approaches to organizational structure and relationships are Edward E. Lawler III, *The Ultimate Advantage: Creating the High Involvement Organization* (San Francisco: Jossey-Bass Publishers, 1992); and Dan Dimancescu, *The Seamless Enterprise: Making Cross-Functional Management Work* (New York: Harper Collins, 1992). The journal *Information Outlook* contains several interesting articles on teams, including two in December 1998: Doris Small Helfer, "Outsourcing, Teaming, and Special Libraries: Threats and Opportunities" and Linda M. McFadden and Kay L. Hubbard, "Team Concepts for Emerging Organizational Architectures."

Chapter 5

Planning and Reporting

Often, when an archivist or archival manager faces a planning "exercise," he or she simply groans about the waste of time. After all, there are collections to process, researchers to assist, and inquiries demanding a response. Who has time for an "exercise" when there is real work to be done? But effective planning is critical for organizational and individual success. If planning is merely an "exercise," then the archival organization will most assuredly be constantly reacting to circumstances rather than anticipating opportunities and challenges.

Planning can suffer from several maladies, any of which may prove fatal. Management in the archives and the larger parent institution must be committed to an effective planning process designed to "drive" the strategies, policies, and budget of the organization. Members of the staff need to be appropriately included in the process so that the organization's culture, often suspicious and resistant to planning efforts, does not smother the effort. Finally, planning must not become a separate bureaucracy unto itself, divorced from the organization and the daily realities of work life. Every archival organization, regardless of its institutional setting, is engaged in a fierce competition for resources and relevancy. Careful planning supports an effective strategy-making process that enables management to meet the requirements of the archives' mission and to obtain the financial, personnel, and other resources needed for success. Careful strategic thinking, planning, and decision making are critical for survival, much less success. Done effectively, planning is at the heart of mission achievement.

Archival Planning

In any organization, including an archives, a wide variety of plans are continually in development and implementation. Plans are used in staffing, budgeting, organizational development, information technology, and facility management to name just a few. This chapter focuses on strategic planning for the archival program and the related operational plans required to implement such a plan and integrate all program activities.

For Henri Fayol it all began with "*pre'voyance,*" by which he meant "foresight, forethought, and prudence." In English the term used is planning. Planning is how an archives attempts to create its future situation by setting goals and strategies to reach those goals. This involves looking ahead with the information available to estimate what is likely to occur using a variety of tools and techniques. In looking to the future, planning focuses on what must be done, not what was or was not achieved in the past. The effectiveness of archival planning depends on the quality of the planning process itself as well as the quality of the strategic thinking and decision making that planning supports.

Most archival organizations exist within a parent institution or structure. Each archives must develop plans and strategies to meet its mission, goals, and objectives and relate them to the direction and purpose of the parent institution. Planning serves as the focal point that integrates all the organization's activities needed to meet the mission and goals of the archives. In broad terms, plans can be short range (one year or less), medium term (one to three years), or long term (three to five years). We will first focus on long-term, or strategic, planning.

Strategic Planning Overview

Strategic planning is a concept and practice deeply embedded in corporate, academic, and governmental institutions. Though strategic

Developing realistic goals and strategies keeps the archives moving in the right direction. Archives Service Center, University Library System, University of Pittsburgh.

planning has it critics, such as Henry Mintzberg, there is a continuing need for effective strategy development and implementation. Regardless of the approach ultimately adopted, some form of strategic thinking and planning must be pursued. There are three ways to create strategy: learning, vision, and planning. All three must be utilized and integrated in any model followed in developing the plan. Several possible models are[1]

Model 1: Top-down approach: the archival organization's senior leaders formulate the strategies and task mid-level managers with developing plans to implement the strategic directions.
Environment: highly centralized and hierarchical organization.

1 Models based on concepts presented by G. Edward Evans, Patricia Layzell Ward, and Bendik Rugaas, *Management Basics for Information Professionals* (New York and London: Neal-Schuman Publishers, 2000), 180–81.

Model 2: MID-LEVEL-UP APPROACH: senior managers prepare general guidance and mid-level managers then develop strategic plans. From the various work products, senior managers create overall strategic plan.
ENVIRONMENT: decentralized organization

Model 3: MIXED APPROACH: Each level of management develops strategies and plans, with overall plan developed after extensive coordination.
ENVIRONMENT: can be used in models 1 and 2 organizations.

Model 4: TEAM APPROACH: staff members and management from all levels work as a team to develop strategies and plans. All employees provided chance for input. Effective in consensus building but slow.
ENVIRONMENT: flat, less hierarchical organizations.

Whatever model or approach is adopted, the first step is to analyze the organization's strengths, weaknesses, opportunities, and threats (SWOT). This analysis must look at political, technological, and sociocultural trends in the external environment: the relationship with the parent institution and with constituent and user groups, and funding, technology, or demographic changes. At the same time, an accurate understanding of the SWOT from the perspective of the internal environment of the organization is also critically important. Factors requiring analysis include the flexibility and adaptability of the archives' organizational culture, its quality of staff, and the strengths and weaknesses in its technical and facility infrastructure.

In conducting the environmental SWOT analysis, input from staff and management, outside experts, and constituent and user groups is necessary to give those leading the planning effort accurate perceptions of the environment. Also, a trained facilitator from outside the organization experienced in strategic planning, preferably in archives, museums, or libraries, must be retained to assist in guiding the strategic planning process. Strategic planning ultimately results in organizational winners and losers, so the services of an objective outside expert is needed to help keep the process honest.

Mission-Vision-Values

The SWOT environment scan is part of the learning methodology in creating strategy. *Vision* and *mission* are also needed to define effective strategies. This means defining at the highest level the organization's reason for existence. What makes the archives unique? Whom does the organization serve? What holdings does the archives acquire, preserve, and provide access to? The vision puts the mission in broader societal terms and purposes. (See figure 5-1.) Finally, the *values* are those that the archival organization seeks to incubate in its employees and in the organization's culture.

Goals, Strategies, and Tasks

After the SWOT analysis is completed and the mission-vision-values are crafted or revised as needed comes the stage of defining what the archives wants to achieve. Strategic goals should be overarching, responsive to the articulated mission and vision, reflective of the opportunities and challenges facing the archives, and indicative of what the organization must achieve to be successful. Strategies are the various avenues pursued to fulfill the strategic goals and may include forging new institutional partnerships, exploiting technology in a different manner, or creating additional sources of funding. Because strategic plans can cover a five- to ten-year time frame, it is necessary to identify objectives or tasks on a yearly basis as measurable milestones toward achieving the goals. (See figure 5-2.) Objectives are assigned to units in the archives, with performance plans for managers and staff tied, at least in part, to achieving the objectives.

Operational Planning

While the strategic plan identifies the major goals and objectives the archives needs to pursue, this is not the full extent of planning required for organizational success. The archives manager must ensure that a yearly operational plan covering all program activities

Figure 5-1 Strategic Plan for Kentucky Department for Libraries and Archives

Mission Statement

The Kentucky Department for Libraries and Archives serves Kentucky's need to know by assuring equitable access to high quality library and information resources and services and by helping public agencies ensure that adequate documentation of government programs is created, efficiently maintained, and made readily accessible.

A Vision for KDLA

A dynamic, evolving organization, the Kentucky Department for Libraries and Archives is a leader in providing quality management and delivery of information resources. It envisions a future in which:

Kentucky is a state whose people have equitable access to the information resources they need for work and home; where government policy and action is well documented and the management of public records promotes government efficiency; and where our libraries are vital partners in the development of this state.

Public libraries are an essential, vibrant element in their communities—places where citizens have unlimited access to a wide variety of information, and are served by well-trained library and archival professionals. With government information readily accessible to citizens, all public agencies are partners with KDLA in meeting documentation and records management responsibilities and have active, ongoing records management programs.

KDLA has forged productive partnerships with these citizens and public agencies, and is known for its staff's strong service orientation, its ability to access a wealth of information resources, and its effective use of technology in all aspects of its work.

(Courtesy of the Kentucky Department for Libraries and Archives)

Figure 5-2 Strategic Initiatives of the Alabama Department of Archives and History

1998–2008
(for FY 2000)

The mission of the Alabama Department of Archives and History is to ensure the preservation of Alabama's historical records and artifacts and to promote a better understanding of Alabama history. In carrying out this mission, the department has a set of core tasks it has managed since 1901. Through this work, the Archives has gathered and seeks to preserve a massive collection of records and artifacts reflecting the history of Alabama.

Now, Alabama is experiencing new economic, technological, and social changes that significantly affect the lives of its citizens and the historical material they produce. These changes also alter the way archives manage, provide access to, and use their historical collections. To continue meeting its responsibilities to the people of the 21st century, the Alabama Department of Archives and History must:

- **provide proper environmental conditions and adequate space for preserving Alabama's historical records and artifacts**
  - complete the west wing addition and restoration of the existing building
    - complete schematics based on information from Lull report (by 12-31-99)
    - investigate fund raising options (Fall 1999)
      –launch fund raising drive (Spring 2000)
    - oversee the detailed architectural work and construction
      –hire project manager
    - deaccession material not within the scope of ADAH's collecting policy
      – establish formal policies for the deaccession process
      – identify material appropriate for deaccession, based on bulk, value, or ease of action

(continued)

Figure 5-2 continued

- **develop information systems that provide electronic access to catalogs of the department's holdings and to widely-used images and data files from the Archives' collections**
  - complete computer cataloging of all material in the department's custody
    - complete collection-level inventory and database of all private records
    - complete inventory of additions to microfilm vault
    - convert all government record finding aids to HTML
    - establish bibliographic control of the book collection
  - implement digital scanning of high-interest indexes and images
    - begin scanning of voter registration records, legislative records, and Confederate muster rolls
    - reassess web services and update web plan
    - implement charge card system

(Courtesy of the Alabama Department of Archives and History)

and functions of the archives is developed. (See figure 5-3.) The operating plan accounts for the hours to be expended for the year ahead by all categories of employees (including volunteers). The plan should also account, by function, for the units of work expected to be accomplished by the staff available. Each program activity or function should be broken into major subcategories that constitute the tasks that must be carried out. The program functions, activities, and subcategories will vary, of course, from archives to archives, but must cover all the life-cycle activities carried out.

In doing strategic and operational planning, there is a very real tendency to take on more than can be realistically accomplished within a given period of time. In preparing the operational plan, the archival manager should carefully correlate staff hours available and operating tasks to be accomplished to see if hours are available for new products or services. If hours are not available in the initial planning effort, then less strategic or less important activities may have to be curtailed or eliminated. Management is all about choices.

Policies and Procedures

After the mission and vision are articulated and the strategic plan is completed, the next step is to develop the policies and procedures that provide the structure and content needed for successful operations. In chapter 4, issues related to developing a policy statement for the archives' mission and key areas of responsibility were discussed. As discussed, a policy is a governing principle that provides overall guidance as to how an archives conducts its business. However, policy guidance is only general in nature and is refined and standardized through the use of specific archival procedures.

Figure 5-3 Operating Plan Concept

Fiscal Year: Organizational Unit:

Table 1—Unit's Available Effective Staff Hours

Type of Employee/Staff	Number of Employees	Total Hours
Permanent Full Time		
Permanent Part Time		
Volunteers		
Unit's Total Staff and Hours		

(continued)

Figure 5-3 continued

Table 2—Operating Plan Hours and Planned Work Units

Function	Staff Hours	Volunteer Hours	Planned Work Units
I. PRESERVATION/HOLDINGS MAINTENANCE			
1. Holdings Maintenance			
2. Lab Services			
3. Preservation Services			
4. SUB-TOTAL (lines 1–3)			
II. REFERENCE			
5. Providing Records			
6. Providing Copies			
7. Direct Responses (oral, written, electronic)			
8. Research Room Activities			
9. Loans			
10. Descriptive Researcher Aids			
11. SUB-TOTAL (lines 5–10)			

(continued)

Figure 5-3 continued

Function	Staff Hours	Volunteer Hours	Planned Work Units
III. PUBLIC PROGRAMS/OUTREACH			
12. Mounting Exhibitions			
13. Loaning Records for Exhibitions			
14. Producing Publications in a Variety of Media			
15. Providing Oral Presentations			
16. Presenting Special Events			
17. Conducting Tours			
18. Public Programs Services			
19. SUB-TOTAL (lines 12–18)			

(continued)

Figure 5-3 continued

Function	Staff Hours	Volunteer Hours	Planned Work Units
IV. ACQUISITIONS AND PROCESSING			
20. Acquisitions Management			
21. Preaccessioning			
22. Archival Accessioning			
23. Initial Processing			
24. Deaccessioning			
25. Space Control			
26. Records Moves and Relocations			
27. SUB-TOTAL (lines 20–26)			
V. TRAINING			
28. Training for Other Units			
29. Internal Archives Training			
30. SUB-TOTAL (lines 28–29)			

(continued)

Figure 5-3 continued

Function	Staff Hours	Volunteer Hours	Planned Work Units
VI. LIBRARY SERVICES			
31. Create Library Collection			
32. Organize Library Collection			
33. Library Use			
34. Maintain Library Collection			
35. SUB-TOTAL (lines 31–34)			
VII. PROGRAM SUPPORT			
36. Program, Administration, and Product Support Activities			
37. SUB-TOTAL (line 36)			
38. FUNCTIONAL ACTIVITIES SUB-TOTAL (lines 4, 11, 19, 27, 30, 35, 37)			
VIII. HOURS AVAILABLE FOR NEW PRODUCTS OR SERVICES			

(Concept courtesy of the National Archives and Records Administration)

Procedures dictating particular courses of action are frequently codified through written manuals, which are often available to staff in hard copy or electronically via an intranet. An access policy, for example, outlines who may use archival collections, when such collections are open for research, and how researchers can gain access to closed collections. Procedures outline how staff members are to deal with researchers when they visit or communicate with the archives. For example, access procedures would cover such issues as how written requests for information (letter, fax, e-mail) should be handled; how the research room will be managed concerning issues such as where the personal belongings of researchers are to be placed, whether researchers must sign a daily register; and what specific steps should be taken when a researcher asks for a restricted collection.

Standardized procedures are an important tool to ensure that staff members carry out their duties in a consistent manner. Manuals can greatly assist the training of new staff members. They also serve as a point of reference when questions arise about how staff members should proceed when dealing with an unfamiliar question or problem. When policies and procedures are created, a period should be set aside to instruct staff members on their use. Such a program may be formal or informal in nature, depending on the size of the repository. An instruction period allows staff members to react to changes in the archives' operation, and staff input may modify and improve the procedures that have been suggested.

Performance Measurement

Any planning effort is only as good as the results. It is vitally important to have a management performance measurement system in place to monitor organizational performance as the work year moves forward. The operating plan statistical report enables the manager to determine if goals and objectives are being met and if there are any trends, problematic or otherwise, that are developing. (See figure 5-4.) This is perhaps the least popular of management tasks and responsibilities, yet it is vital that a simple, effective system be put in place and used. The act of translating vision or strategy into measurable

Figure 5-4 Operating Plan Statistical Report—Concept

Organizational Unit *Month* *Prepared by*

I. PRESERVATION	Hours		Work Units Completed	
	Staff	**Volunteer**	**Staff/Vol.**	**Contractor**
1. Holdings Maintenance				
2. Lab Services				
3. Preservation Services				
4. PRESERVATION TOTAL (lines 1–3)				

II. REFERENCE	Hours		Work Units Completed	
	Staff	**Volunteer**	**Staff/Vol.**	**Contractor**
5. Providing Records				
6. Providing Copies				
7. Direct Responses				
8. Research Room Activities				
9. Loans				
10. Descriptive Research Aids				
11. REFERENCE TOTALS (lines 5–10)				

(continued)

Figure 5-4 continued

III. PUBLIC PROGRAMS	HOURS		WORK UNITS COMPLETED	
	Staff	Volunteer	Staff/Vol.	Contractor
12. Mounting Exhibitions				
13. Loaning Records for Exhibitions				
14. Producing Publications in a Variety of Media				
15. Providing Oral Presentations				
16. Presenting Film Series; Performances; Special Events				
17. Conducting Tours				
18. Public Programs Services				
19. PUBLIC PROGRAMS TOTAL (lines 12–18)				

(continued)

Figure 5-4 continued

IV. ACQUISITION AND PROCESSING	Hours		Work Units Completed	
	Staff	Volunteer	Staff/Vol.	Contractor
20. Acquisitions Management				
21. Preaccessioning				
22. Archival Accessioning				
23. Initial Processing				
24. Deaccessioning				
25. Space Control				
a. Space Control—Records				
b. Space Control—Staff and other Nonrecords Storage Needs				
26. Records Moves and Relocations				
27. RECORDS LIFE CYCLE TOTAL (lines 20–26)				

(continued)

Figure 5-4 continued

V. TRAINING	Hours		Work Units Completed	
	Staff	Volunteer	Staff/Vol.	Contractor
28. Training for Other Units				
29. Internal Archival Training				
30. TRAINING TOTAL (lines 20–26)				

VI. LIBRARY SERVICES	Hours		Work Units Completed	
	Staff	Volunteer	Staff/Vol.	Contractor
31. Create Library Collection				
32. Organize Library Collection				
33. Library Use				
34. Maintain Library Collection				
35. LIBRARY SERVICES TOTAL (lines 31–34)				

(continued)

Figure 5-4 continued

VII. SUPPORT ACTIVITIES	Hours		Work Units Completed	
	Staff	**Volunteer**	**Staff/Vol.**	**Contractor**
36. Program, Administration, and Product Support				
a. Program support activities				
b. Administrative support activities				
c. Product support activities				
37. SUPPORT ACTIVITIES TOTALS (lines 36 a–c)				
VIII. OTHER ACTIVITIES	**Hours**		**Work Units Completed**	
	Staff	**Volunteer**	**Staff/Vol.**	**Contractor**
38. Training Taken and Professional Activities				
39. Labor Activities				
40. EEO and Similar Activities				
41. Miscellaneous				
42. Leave & Holidays				
43. OTHER ACTIVITIES TOTALS (lines 38–42)				
56. ALL ACTIVITIES TOTALS (lines 4+11+19+27 +3-+35+37+43)				

(Concept courtesy of the National Archives and Records Administration)

objectives forces specificity and surfaces hidden disagreements that require resolution.

Traditionally, measurement and reporting systems focused more on quantity in the form of outputs than on quality. Yet all sectors of society now proclaim the value of quality in organizational performance. This can take a wide variety of forms depending on the organization or activity under discussion. Like all other entities, archives have customer expectations to meet, collections to process, and holdings to preserve. All of these requirements must often be met with limited time, staff, and other resources. So, inadequate reference responses, poorly processed collections, and deteriorating records are costly in every sense of the term.

Quality work is the only answer. Work must be done well the first time. Measuring this is not easy. One way to start is to incorporate quality standards into the archives' procedures. Further quality of work must be included in the performance measurement system. Quality can be measured. For example, standards can be developed for the extent of research to be undertaken in response to a reference inquiry and the elements that must be included in a quality response. Managers can use auditing or sampling techniques to review reference responses for adherence to quality standards. Of course, quality standards can be set for other aspects of archival work such as processing or preservation activities. Quality standards should be incorporated into standardized procedures and incorporated into individual or team performance standards.

Organizational, team, and individual performance can be measured objectively only through use of a reliable performance measurement system. Managers should require statistical reports as regularly as the work demands. This could be on a weekly, monthly, quarterly, or even semi-annual basis. The timing depends upon the situation. This focus on measurement aids in aligning organizational efforts and nurturing a culture of teamwork. Performance plans for teams and individual staff members are based on strategic and operating plan requirements as well as the job elements defined in job descriptions prepared at the time of hiring, recruitment, and selection. (See chapter 8 on the human resources management aspects of performance plans.)

Keeping Current

All plans need updating if they are to remain effective organizational and management tools. Both strategic and operating plans require at least a yearly review, with strategic plans needing a comprehensive review and possible overhaul every three to five years. Project plans (see chapter 6), of course, may well require adjustments on a more frequent basis. But all plans are subject to various exigencies that can arise. The effective manager is flexible and can adapt strategies and plans to sometimes rapidly changing environments.

As with the creation of plans, keeping current should involve all staff members to a greater or lesser extent depending on circumstances. Staff commitment is essential to achieve the success the various planning tools are designed to accomplish. So, the manager's task is to keep the staff involved, enthusiastic, and committed.

Conclusion

Planning is one of the most important management tasks. Planning is not an exercise, it is rather the lifeblood of the archives. No matter how small or large, the archives must make effective plans to help steer the program, which must be integrated into the planning of the parent institution. Managers fight to get their unit's tasks and responsibilities into institutional strategic and operating plans because in a very real sense if they are not in the plan, they may cease to exist. Hopefully, this chapter has purged the idea that planning is an academic, time-wasting task. For if that is what is happening, then real planning has not taken place.

Suggested Readings

G. Edward Evans, et al., in *Management Basics for Information Professionals,* provides a good overview of the planning process (chapter 7) with a detailed and comprehensive bibliography. Other useful general works include Peter Drucker, *Management: Tasks, Responsibilities, and Practices;* and Henry Mintzberg, *The Rise and Fall of Strategic Planning* (New York: Prentice Hall, 1994). Mintzberg does a good job of exploring the weaknesses in strategic planning, particularly on how the concept is actually applied by various types of organizations. For a basic understanding of the intersection of management, performance, and measurement, consult Mark T. Czarnecki, *Managing by Measuring: How to Improve Your Organization's Performance Through Effective Benchmarking* (New York: American Management Association, 1999).

A still useful example of a planning document is the Society of American Archivists, *Planning for the Archival Profession, A Report of the SAA Task Force on Goals and Priorities* (Chicago: Society of American Archivists, 1986). Other sources can be located on the Internet, including the strategic plans and initiatives of the National Archives and Records Administration, state archives, and various corporations such as J. C. Penney.

CHAPTER 6

Project Management

When this revision of the manual was under consideration, a number of archivists requested that the topic of project management be included. This is not surprising as many, if not most archivists, will be involved in multiple projects over the span of their careers. One of the themes for this manual is the critical importance of teamwork and collaborative work efforts. A successful project requires effective teamwork, so the two concepts are inextricably woven together. Because of the nature of archival work, archives are always in the midst of creating, implementing, or completing projects. A successful archivist must understand the project concept and how to manage projects throughout what is termed the "project life cycle." Managers whose work encompasses significant project management responsibilities should consult the publications and services provided by the Project Management Institute. (See appendix on Management Literature, Web Sites, and Professional Associations for further information.)

What Is a Project?

The Project Management Institute defines a project as "a temporary endeavor undertaken to create a unique product or service." Management author John Nicholas adds a few elements and defines a project as having "a single, definable purpose, end product or result, usually

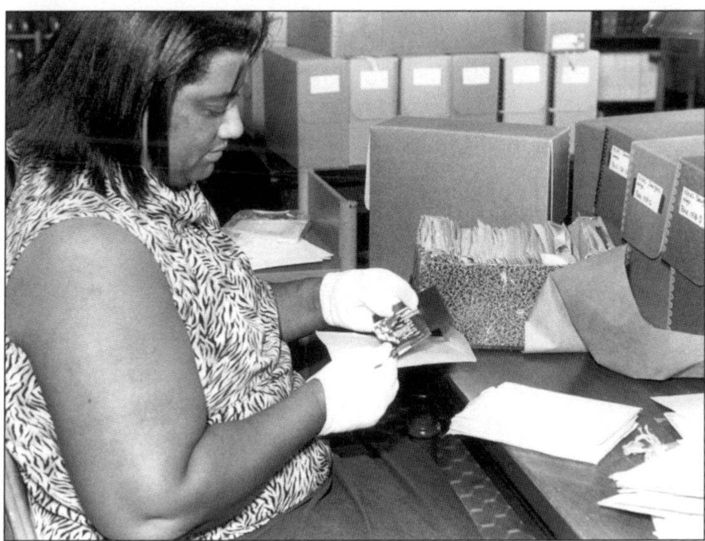

Processing collections. AUSTIN HISTORY CENTER, AUSTIN PUBLIC LIBRARY

specified in terms of cost, schedule, and performance requirements."[1] Projects are really building blocks in the design and execution of an organization's strategic goals and objectives. Projects often involve a matrix management where horizontal teams pulled together from across organizational boundaries are grafted on, for a time, to the vertical hierarchical structure. Projects by definition are temporary, finite, and goal oriented. All projects operate within resource boundaries, organizational constraints, and other factors that must be appropriately managed to achieve success. Projects may or may not have an information technology component. If they do, this may introduce a unique set of problems, task interdependencies, and software and hardware configurations.

Project Management

Broadly speaking, project management involves the overall context in which the project takes place (i.e., organizational environment, role of

1 John M. Nicholas, *Managing Business and Engineering Projects: Concepts and Implementation* (Englewood Cliffs, N.J.: Prentice Hall, 1990), 11.

stakeholders); scope management and planning; human resources management; and integrating the project into the products, services, and work process of the organization. Organizational environment will obviously impact the chances of a project's success. If senior management is disengaged or adequate resources are not provided, the chances for a project reaching its goals are remote. Managers must work together to positively channel psychic energy involving turf issues, technical or professional concerns, or anxiety about change.

Stakeholder issues are also potentially significant for project management. Stakeholders are individuals or groups who have some kind of stake in the project's outcome. In a project to design an electronic recordkeeping system, for example, those who will use the system obviously have a stake in the project. In a project to design and implement an automated finding aid, stakeholders would include researchers as well as staff who will have to populate the finding aid and use it to answer reference inquiries. Stakeholders, in other words, are those people with some sort of official (or contractual) relationship to the project and those with an informal but nonetheless real interest. Stakeholder opposition or confusion about a project can greatly impede the project. It is important to get stakeholder input when developing project requirements and to provide updates as the project progresses. If the project has an IT product or service as its deliverable, then demos at various stages in development and design would be very useful.

Because projects and project teams are temporary, cross functional, and operate under tight time and logistical constraints, a clear understanding of roles and responsibilities within the organization is critical for success. The project manager, quite often an archivist, must identify from various areas of the archives or from the parent institution team members with the needed skills and expertise required to achieve the goals of the project. The project manager must negotiate with managers of units that will be affected by the project for support and resources needed to achieve project goals. The project manager must plan the project and integrate schedule, costs, and tasks. Most importantly, the leadership qualities of the project manager can be essential to the success of the project team. Archivists who are going to work as project or team leaders need training in decision making, consensus building, conflict resolution, and systems thinking. The project manager needs to develop these skills not only to lead the team but to deal with unit managers and the organization's senior management.

The project team is another ingredient critical for project success. The individuals selected for the team must not only have the needed skills and expertise, but they must also be committed to the goals of the project. Projects can be intense and stressful, and a common commitment to the task is essential for team cohesiveness. As with the project manager, team members need training to develop the ability to make group decisions, resolve conflicts, and perform their tasks.

Project need and scope are often directed by the archives' or parent institution's senior management. This top-down situation can create tension within the organization at large. Senior management must provide the project team with the support and resources needed to accomplish the task. The project, which may affect one or more elements of the archives' mission, can be sensitive and potentially stir up "turf" conflicts. Senior management and the project manager must work closely with all affected units and managers to resolve conflicts that, if left unmanaged, may destroy the possibility of project success.

The most critical task in project management is effective communication. All projects, regardless of size, are most likely to contain at least certain elements of complexity, require change, and intrude on previously existing organizational relationships. If all aspects of project management but communication are professionally executed, the possibility of failure is greatly increased. A formal, well-thought-out communication strategy is strongly recommended. This would include a communication plan for the project team, for other units and managers affected by the project, and for any external constituencies with an interest in the project. Effective communication serves several useful purposes. Ongoing communication helps identify potential roadblocks or opposition, as well as areas requiring coordination, and it can aid with the buy-in. It takes time to develop a communication plan and to do the communicating. But, failing to do this guarantees a problematic project.

Project Life Cycle

Projects, like records, have a life cycle. (See figure 6-1.) Nicholas identifies four stages: conception, definition, acquisition, and operation. In the conception stage, the principal actors, usually the institution's senior management, take the initiative in identifying the need for a project and determine its feasibility. The project manager and the team are constituted and any training needed is provided.

In the second stage, the definition phase, the project is clearly defined as to scope, goals, and required resources. (See figure 6-2.) At this planning phase, the system(s) that the project will affect must be clearly identified and analyzed for potential positive and negative impact. For example, a project designed to revise the institution's acquisition or accessioning policy and procedures will directly affect processing, conservation, and, ultimately, reference or access. Realistic project milestones and time-lines must also be established and incorporated into the plan. In this phase, user and system requirements must be clearly enunciated. Failure to do so will ensure that whatever the goal (i.e., product or service), it will not meet the needs of the organization. Information technology projects in particular can founder on this point. Understanding such processes and customer needs, and then defining performance requirements, are critical components in achieving the project's goals. Resource planning, scheduling, and breaking down the work to be done are all key elements in the second stage.

The third stage, acquisition, includes the actual design of the project based on the definition of the project and the requirements identified. In this stage, the project is actually carried out and implemented.* Project evaluation and progress (see figure 6-3) are critical to ensure that the project remains on schedule, within budget, and moving forward to achieve the goals defined for the project. During this phase, continued stakeholder involvement is critical. Meeting expectations is the value-added component to the project that are arguably equal to or more significant than schedule and budget.

---

* Acquisition involves setting up panels to evaluate vendors' bids from technical and cost perspectives. Panels should include members familiar with the technical requirements and with the expertise to evaluate cost proposals.

Figure 6-1 Project Life Cycle

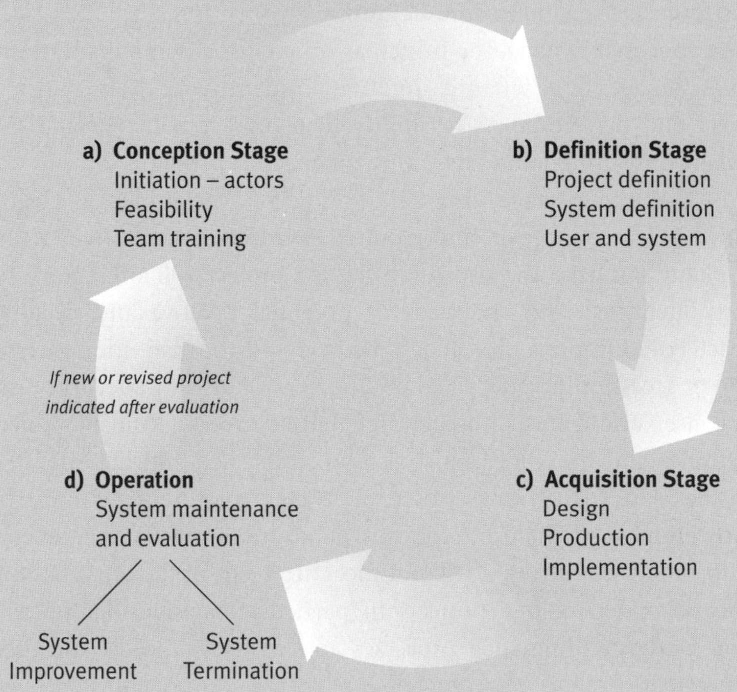

a) **Conception Stage**
Initiation – actors
Feasibility
Team training

b) **Definition Stage**
Project definition
System definition
User and system

c) **Acquisition Stage**
Design
Production
Implementation

d) **Operation**
System maintenance
and evaluation

System
Improvement

System
Termination

If new or revised project indicated after evaluation

(Courtesy of Pearson Education, Inc. Chart found in Nicholas, Managing Business and Engineering Projects, *92.)*

Figure 6-2 Project Plan

1. **Project Identification:** Provide the name of the project and any other identifying information needed for clarity and later tracking.
2. **Project Manager:** Name of the individual empowered and accountable for the successful completion of the project.
3. **Project Concept:** In a brief narrative (three to five paragraphs), describe the organizational (business) needs and customer requirements that the project will address and resolve. Describe how the project will address the identified needs and requirements. Cite any overarching strategic plan or initiative of the archives or parent institution that impinges on the project.
4. **Major Tasks:** Identify the major tasks (usually five to eight) that must be accomplished to successfully complete the project. Identify who will be responsible for completing the overall project and each task, such as a team, unit, or contractor. Tasks and subtasks should be broken into specific milestones. For complex projects, project management tools such as the Gantt chart should be used.
5. **Resource Requirements:** Provide an estimate of the staff hours and contractor costs, if any, needed to complete the project. Also, include all other resource needs such as equipment, supplies, training, and space. Source(s) of funding should also be indicated. The acquisition strategy for all goods and services needed to accomplish the tasks must be identified.
6. **Strategies:** Identify alternative strategies to accomplish the goals of the project and justify the recommended approach. Include all known concerns and constraints that could affect the project.
7. **Risk Management Plan:** Identify all risks that represent the greatest threats to the project's timetable and budget. For each risk identified, assess the likelihood of its taking place and describe the strategy intended to mitigate the risk.

(Concept courtesy of the National Archives and Records Administration)

Figure 6-3 Project Management Progress Report

1. **Reporting period:** Can cover any desired period of time, e.g., weekly, monthly, quarterly.
2. **Project:** Include the name and any required identification, such as the project number or budget code.
3. **Milestones:** A milestone represents an event or condition that marks the completion of a part of the project. Indicate tasks from the project plan that are considered milestones and anticipated completion dates. Discuss the project status in relation to the allotted time for completion. Is the project ahead of schedule, on schedule, or behind schedule? As appropriate, indicate the time adjustments to the project that are required to complete the project successfully.
4. **Costs:** Discuss the project status in relation to the anticipated costs. Is the project under or over budget?
   a. **Contractor costs:** Discuss the costs, if any, that have been obligated for contractor support and if any additional funds will be required to complete the project. Explain completely the reasons for the additional funds, as appropriate.
   b. **Staff costs:** Discuss the costs or staff hours that have been expended on the project. Will more staff costs or hours than estimated be required to complete the project? Use only existing sources or information to determine staff hours and costs.
5. **Achievements:** Describe any successes or achievements of the project thus far. In particular, indicate events that should be communicated to staff, other parts of the institution, or the public.
6. **Problems:** Describe any concerns involving the project, including resource availability, unanticipated snags, contractor issues, stakeholder resistance, changes in priorities, etc. Serious concerns should be reported as soon as identified and not held until the formal report is submitted.
7. **Other:** Provide any additional information that may be helpful to determine the status of the project.

(Concept courtesy of the National Archives and Records Administration)

The final, or operation, stage involves completing the project and establishing a feedback mechanism to evaluate over the long term the product or service created as a result of the project. Evaluation will lead to system improvement over time, or may, in certain cases, result in terminating a particular product or service.

Project as System

As previously noted, projects invariably have an impact on existing systems of operation and organization. But the project itself is also a system of people and resources integrated, organized, and managed to achieve its goals. So, the project manager and the team must understand the project as a system and manage all its parts and relationships accordingly. In looking at the project and its impact, the manager and the team must identify the big picture, the complex whole with all of its parts, which interact in a coordinated way to make up the system.

For example, most archives permit copies of records to be made for research purposes. Thus, most institutions will have some sort of an order fulfillment system. The parts of such a system include archivists, conservators (for fragile records), accountants (financial controls) and, in many cases, information technology staff if the system is automated. And, of course, researchers are also part of the system. A project to devise a new order fulfillment system or even to change just one component must look at the big picture to understand how the whole system operates and the interrelationship of its parts.

Regardless of the type or size of the project, a number of methodologies are available for systems or project management. These include systems analysis, systems engineering, and systems management. While complex methodologies may not be needed or appropriate for all projects, the basic principles apply. These involve looking at an entire work process or system and understanding how all parts or systems relate to one another. When analyzing a process or system, the project manager and the team must understand how a change in one part of the system affects other parts (systems thinking). For example, a change in the pricing structure may impact the number of copies made and this will have an impact on other parts of the system. Another principle utilizes problem solving (systems analysis) as the basic project tool or methodology. Problem solving includes understanding requirements and project objectives, setting criteria for making decisions, and examining alternative strategies to achieve the desired goals of the project.

If the project manager and the team do not take a holistic approach to the project, the chances of achieving the desired result are markedly diminished.

Risk Management

Risk management may be the most overlooked element of project management. After all, what could go wrong with a good project manager, team, and plan? Plenty can go wrong, much of it unanticipated. Risk management means systematically identifying at the beginning of the project events that could occur to the detriment of the project and preparing a strategy to respond. After this is done, several analytical factors are brought into play. First, determine how likely the event or risk is to occur. Then, the severity of the consequences if the event occurs needs to be quantified. After risks have been identified, assessed, and quantified, a response must be developed for each threat, in order of priority. Each problem has several solutions. Finally, documentation of the risk management strategies needs to be pulled together and made available to management and the project team if the need arises.

It is useful to get input from stakeholders and others in the organization as the risk management strategy is being developed. The project team alone does not possess the sum of all knowledge and imagination. The project manager needs the best strategies and alternative solutions available in case a threat should arise. A well–thought-out risk management plan could actually instill confidence in stakeholders and others in the organization.

Factors for Success

To summarize, there are five factors for success in a project management endeavor:

1. Mandate: The project, the project manager, and the team must receive a clear mandate from the senior management to undertake the task. The charge must be clear, unambiguous, and straightforward about the desired result.
2. Support/Resources: Adequate time, materials, and other resources must be made available for project success. This includes dealing with organizational or cultural restraints that pose a barrier to the project.
3. Team Leadership/Facilitation: The project manager must have the necessary technical and interpersonal skills needed for project achievement. Team members must also be chosen with the same set of criteria. All members must receive any training needed to work effectively, particularly in regard to systems thinking and analysis.
4. Communication: It is vital that the project's timetable include ample time for communication and feedback with senior management, other managers, and users or customers. Among other things, regular communication can be an "early warning system" to alert the project team to potential problems.
5. Clear Goals: The project must have very clear, attainable goals along with a detailed and comprehensive project plan.

Conclusion

Every archival manager needs to acquire project management skill. Attending workshops or seminars in project management offered by the Project Management Institute or the American Management Association, or taking courses at local colleges or universities are the best ways to acquire the knowledge needed for effective project management. Potential project managers should first serve on teams as apprentices to more experienced project managers and thereby learn the ropes firsthand. But when all is said and done, there is no escape from learning through trial and error. Any manager with several projects under her or his belt will gain not only experience but confidence as well.

Suggested Readings

Several works by John M. Nicholas provide a helpful overview of projects and project management. These include *Project Management for Business and Technology: Principles and Practice* (Englewood Cliffs, N.J.: Prentice-Hall, 2001); and *Managing Business and Engineering Projects: Concepts and Implementation* (Englewood Cliffs, N.J.: Prentice-Hall, 1990). While geared to business and engineering, these texts do provide a basic understanding of the project life cycle and contain illustrations that can be adapted by the archival manager. MacKenzie Kyle, *Making It Happen: A Non-technical Guide to Project Management* (Toronto: John Wiley and Sons/Canada Ltd., 1998) provides a good, basic primer that defines the concept of a project and deals with team dynamics, project phases, users' needs, quality, and cost. The Project Management Institute has published Jeffrey K. Pinto, ed., *Project Management Handbook* (San Francisco: Jossey-Bass, 1998). This lengthy and detailed compendium will provide any archival manager with more than enough information on project management.

At the SAA annual meeting in August 1999, the Management Roundtable sponsored a session entitled "Getting the Job Done: Project Management for Archivists." The paper presented by Daria D'Arienzo, "More Than a 'To Do List': Putting the Project in Context," provides a brief, overall framework for project management.

Chapter 7

Managing Information Technology

The key managerial task is to acquire and appropriately use resources to achieve the mission of the organization. From the archival perspective, resources include personnel, space and equipment, funding, and the archival holdings themselves. Perhaps the most difficult resource to manage is information technology, which is rapidly coming centerstage in archival operations regardless of their size. Managers are often intimidated by the technical complexities, jargon, and rapid changes that characterize information technology. Experts maintain that the life cycle for systems and applications is approximately eighteen months before obsolescence sets in and a new cycle begins. Archival managers cannot expect to become experts in the information technology arena. But a clear perspective on the role and place of information technology in the archival enterprise will assist them in making prudent and appropriate decisions.

Information technology is basically a tool, like other tools, designed to assist in planning, decision making, program support, and customer service. All management tools or instruments must be designed and implemented to carry out the archives' mission (effectiveness) in the most businesslike manner (efficiency). All tools and instruments must be evaluated on the basis of these two fundamental criteria. This is particularly critical given the cost and complexity of information technology.

Management Imperative

The evolution of computer technology from mainframes to fourth-generation microcomputers, accompanied by the communications revolution spawned by the World Wide Web and the Internet, forces every archival manager to confront and appropriately exploit information technology, both from an internal, operational perspective and from the external, environmental perspective. As part of a larger organization, an archives often must communicate via electronic mail and transmit fiscal, statistical, and operational data to other components of the parent institution. Demands for the collection, analysis, and transmission of data are ever increasing.

Furthermore, customers expect to have immediate or nearly immediate access to the archives' services and holdings by means of Web technology. (See chapter 9 for further discussion on Web technology and communications.) The very relevance of the archives itself is at stake with high internal and external expectations for access to information. Managers need access to data for day-to-day operations to be able to schedule work, track hours worked, and quantify units of work completed. Whether in the public or private sector, archival managers must justify the effectiveness and efficiency of their programs, and automated management systems have increasingly become a requirement of doing business. From an external and more visible perspective, archives are often expected to provide automated access to catalogs of holdings, series descriptions, reference inquiries, and on-line ordering of products. Our "wired" world with "24/7" service expectations and on-line access to almost any conceivable product, service, or item of information has set very high user expectations.

The fundamental imperative for the archival manager is to understand how customer needs, program requirements, and information technology fit together.[1] Because archives are situated within the broader environment of the parent institution, they are affected by the profound changes in the way in which organizations create, utilize,

1 Various chapters in this manual deal with information technology. In particular, see chapters 3, 4, 5, and 9 for the role of information technology in organizational relationships, planning, communications, and management theory and practice.

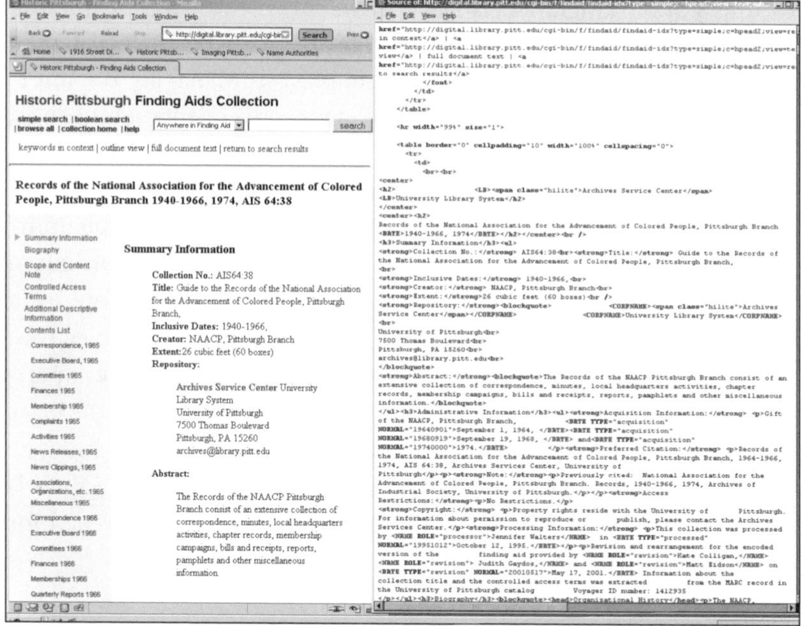

EAD finding aids enable archives to make their collections more widely available to more researchers and let researchers work when the archives is closed.
ARCHIVES SERVICE CENTER, UNIVERSITY LIBRARY SYSTEM, UNIVERSITY OF PITTSBURGH

store, and dispose of information. In this knowledge management environment, archivists bring to the organization and to information technology skills in understanding the relationship between records creators and records, an appreciation of the basic archival principles of provenance and original order, putting information in context, and recordkeeping requirements needed to ensure the authenticity and reliability of records.

The archival manager needs to bring together archival skills and knowledge about records and records systems with information technology. For example, the ways in which records are appraised and scheduled, described, and made available are increasingly affected by information technology. The Web and the distinctive mark-up language used (Hyper Text Marking Language, HTML) are directly useful for marking or tagging documents and display. Canadian archivist Jean-Stephen Piché ties together the Web, Web browsers, and tagged documents this way: "This is particularly important for archives because it provides the ability to link hypertext documents together in various ways through hyperlinks and thereby provide a context or an environment in which many disparate files can be interrelated in meaningful ways."[2] This capability can assist in managing the information of the parent institution by linking records retention schedules, records description, and finding aids for reference use.

To manage in such an environment, the archival manager must engage, above all else, in systematic information technology planning and decision making. It is imperative, though, that all information technology planning, development, and implementation flow from the archives' or parent institution's mission, goals, and objectives. This is critical to avoid becoming entangled with technology experts or mesmerized by the latest options, generally losing sight of the basic operational and program requirements that must drive technology development. Archivists are expected to know their core business needs and requirements and to be able to communicate what is needed for effective and efficient operations.

Planning, Products, and Processes

Planning and decision-making processes for information technology can, of necessity, be quite complex and at certain stages require computer specialists and information systems analysts and designers. At the core, though, effective planning focuses on customers, products, and related work processes. (See figures 7-1 and 7-2.) An organization's strategic or long-range plan should identify the archives' internal and external customers, their product needs, and service requirements; and it should provide the basis for information technology designed to achieve the organization's goals, objectives, and tasks. As stated previously, a strategic or long-range plan clearly states the archives' mission, vision, overarching goals, and measurable objectives and tasks. At the core of the plan, customers, constituents, and information products or services required to meet demands and expectations should be clearly identified.

---

2 Jean-Stephen Piché, "Doing What's Possible with What We've Got: Using the World Wide Web to Integrate Archival Functions," *American Archivist* 61 (Spring 1998): 108.

Figure 7-1 Overview of the Seven Planning and Decision-Making Processes

1. **Long-Range Planning** identifies your customers, describes the purpose of your organization, outlines goals, and identifies products and services to meet customers' needs.
2. **Product Planning and Management** detail the products and services identified in the long-range plan, including the life cycle of the product from inception to retirement. An example of a product that might be identified in the long-range plan is a system for providing archival finding aids.
3. **Business Process Architecture** identifies the processes that will produce the products and services described above. Three examples of business processes are appraising, providing access to, and storing archival records.
4. **Information Technology Strategy and Tactics** determine what approach the organization will take in applying technology to the business processes and products.
5. **Information Technology Strategy and Tactics** establish the principles upon which hardware and software will be selected, specifies technology standards, defines databases, and describes how the technology-related processes and products work together.
6. **Hardware, Software, and Communication Choices** identify what hardware and software to use and establish the procedures for determining whether to buy or develop systems.
7. **Application Acquisition and Development** define the process used to buy or develop an application.

(Courtesy of the International Council on Archives)

Figure 7-2 Planning and Decision-Making Process

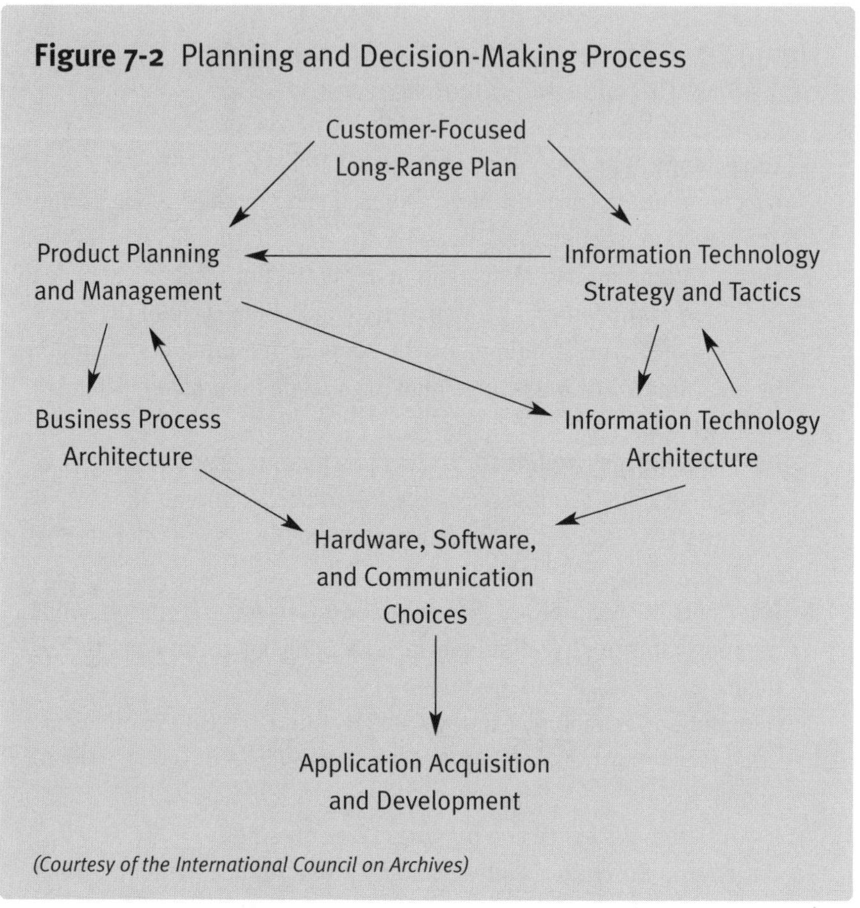

(Courtesy of the International Council on Archives)

"Products" in this context usually refer to archival or informational needs that are met through the design and implementation of information technology systems. Examples include systems for archival finding aids, on-line access to digitized or electronic records, or the workflow management of archival life cycle processes. After the identification of product needs, the next step is to create a product plan. Product plans, according to the International Council on Archives, "define the life cycle of each product from inception through retirement, justify the products relationship to other products, and describe how all products work together." It should be noted that the rigor of the product planning process is also useful for nonautomated products or services. A well-crafted product plan (see figure 7-3) identifies the customer requirements, all steps required to produce and maintain the product, and the life-cycle cost of the product. As outlined by the ICA's Committee on Automation, the key elements of a product plan include[3]

- A description of the product, its features, and its life cycle from inception and maintenance through retirement.
- A description of the product's customers, including their need for the product.
- The product's relationship to other products and how all will work together.
- The product's potential impact on the organization and other customers.
- The budget and other resources needed.
- The product justification and cost benefit analysis—sometimes called a business case.
- How the product or service will be marketed.
- How to provide customer support
- A description of security concerns.

Regardless of the size of the institution, product planning and management are critical tools in producing what customers need and require. For complex products or services, particularly those involving information technology, a team is required. Experts in subject matter or service content must work with technology specialists in designing and implementing the product. However, the archivist, as the product owner, must have ultimate responsibility for the product to ensure that user needs, not just technology concerns alone, drive the entire project.

With a clear sense of customer needs and desired products and services comes the need for effective work processes to support the enterprise. Keeping product or service requirements in mind, work processes should be clear, simple, and holistically conceived so that the desired products or services are indeed provided. For example,

3 International Council on Archives, Committee on Archival Automation, *Planning for Information Technology in Archives: Planning and Decision Processes*, 1996, 5.

Figure 7-3 Information Technology Product Plan Model

	Element	*Description*
1.	**Name of Application**	Proposed product, service, or system title.
2.	**Product Owner**	Senior archivist or manager who will "own" the product for life-cycle management.
3.	**Business Problem**	Background information on the problem or situation that the proposed product will address. Includes statements on business and needs driving the need for the product. Links to the organization's strategic or long-range goals should be clearly stated.
4.	**Proposed IT Solution**	The description of the proposed application indicates how business and customers' needs will be addressed, along with savings and benefits to the organization, relationships to other IT applications, and risks.
5.	**Coordination and Impact**	Identifies all other organizational partners and the coordination required to successfully develop the application.
6.	**Resources Required**	Estimates of staff, contractor, software, and hardware costs.
7.	**Alternatives**	Analysis of alternatives to the proposed solution, along with costs, benefits, and risks for each alternative.
8.	**Implementation Plan**	Overall project milestones from the beginning of product development to implementation.

(Concept courtesy of the National Archives and Records Administration)

when developing an automated access tool or descriptive program, all the steps in the relevant work processes must be examined, modified, or discarded as needed and redesigned to support an automated application and to maximize the benefits from automation. Again, a small team from the archival and information technology staffs, under the guidance of the archives' manager, is the best way to re-engineer work processes.

IT Strategy and Tactics

Information technology strategy flows from the long-range plan, identified products or sources, and simplified, effective work processes. Archival managers and others in the parent institution must be the driving forces behind the information technology strategy as the basic decisions are program based rather than technical. Most archives are not on the cutting edge of the technology continuum. Rather, most have to use existing technologies and applications.

That being the case, managers must understand their organization's attitude toward technology and the funding support available to support systems. They must also understand the organization's technological capabilities. For example, is there an integrated, automated life-cycle information system in place? What is the capacity of the personal computers available for staff and customers? Is a client-server approach with connections to the Web in use or planned?

In other words, the archival manager must sufficiently understand the information system architecture in place to determine if the available technology and applications will restrict or hinder end-users and staff in day-to-day operations and the providing of products and services. In most cases, trade-offs will have to be made. When managers become involved with information technology staff in developing a system, it is vital that to the greatest extent possible an open system technology architecture be adopted rather than a proprietary system. Open systems using commercial off-the-shelf (COTS) products have greater flexibility for dealing with long-term issues of data migration and integration.

Systems Development

The archival manager, as the owner of the product or service in development or revision, must confront architecture issues involving hardware, software, databases, and standards. The hardware, software, and communications choices first lead to the basic decision of whether to buy or develop systems, and then to the actual process of application acquisition and development. The archival manager, unless he or she is also an expert in information technology, can truly feel at sea at this point. The key point is to stay focused on the customer or staff needs and the products or services required to meet the goals and strategies of the organization's long-range or strategic plan.

At this point in the information technology process, the archival manager will be working very closely with in-house technical staff or contractors. As the archival manager works with technical staff to deal with questions related to data and technology architecture and standards, the need for staff and customers to deal with compatible systems based on international or industry standards must be paramount. It is critical that the team explore and document all viable alternatives so that the most appropriate solution is selected for developing the system. Also, archival managers should be aware of various standards applicable to systems development such as ISO/IEC 12207, Software Lifecycle Processes; ISO/IEC TR 15271:1998, Information Technology Guide for Software Lifecycle Processes; and ISO/IEC TR 16326:1999, Software Engineering Guide for the application of ISO/IEC 12207 to project management.

The goals in creating hardware, software, and communications systems are to have as few systems as possible to meet customer/product needs and for these systems to be integrated with any existing systems so that information transfer can be made as easily and inexpensively as possible. Issues of which vendors or applications to select flow from all the decisions made in earlier stages. The archival manager should be part of the team of IT specialists, program analysts, and others who select vendors. All archival or information requirements must be included along with other system requirements and performance expectations in the request for proposals issued to potential bidders. These requirements and performance standards (e.g., how quickly a system should respond to an inquiry) form the basis for evaluating proposals, ranking bidders, and selecting the vendor most suitable for the task. An archival manager or an expert from the archival staff must be involved at every stage—from design through acquisition to implementation.

Implementation

IT management doesn't end with system acquisition and implementation. The archival manager has to ensure that the institution has a plan in place for the maintenance and ongoing operations. This involves the cost of staff or contractor support, equipment refreshment needed over time, and training for staff or other users.

In many ways, the most difficult challenge for the archival manager comes with the introduction of a product or service involving information technology. Issues involving resistance to change and training needs come to the fore during the implementation phase. Resistance occurs for a variety of reasons. Some staff can feel unfamiliar or threatened by the introduction of a new system. For others, particularly in management, information technology can be perceived as a threat to status or power. Yet, it is just as true that information technology can be a liberating tool and the means for supporting personal development and achievement. For all involved, a new system requires mastering new techniques and processes and, at least initially, can make work more complex.

There are a number of strategies to cope with this situation. As discussed in chapter 8, teaming can be an effective tool for improving work processes and the quality of products and services, and it can enhance the capability and morale of staff. Clearly, the planning and decision-making processes require teamwork both within the archival staff and with technical staff that may or may not be within the archives' organizational structure. The sense of involvement and control is critical for the buy-in needed for information technology systems. Getting all those affected by the change involved from the beginning is critical for success.

Another strategy for change management is training. Whether a new system is being implemented for all staff, or an application for just a few, or new staff members need orientation, effective training is vitally important. This can range from system documentation and user manuals to one-on-one mentoring to sophisticated technologies such as multicasting and video-on-demand. The scale of the system being implemented, the openness of the staff, and the resources available for training all will determine the actions needed to ensure success at the implementation stage. Training must not be an afterthought. Training needs should be identified at the beginning of any systems development to achieve the greatest impact.

Conclusion

When it comes to information technology, the greatest challenge for the archival manager is to avoid getting overwhelmed or flustered. After all, effective managers know their business, their customers' needs, and the products and work processes required to meet those needs. Using common sense and keeping a clear focus on program requirements will greatly enhance the chances for success.

The key concept for the archival manager in the information technology enterprise to practice is "partnership," specifically with in-house technical staff or contractors. Horror stories abound about disastrous system implementations. Working effectively with information technology specialists is essential to avoid these. As the old adage puts it, "Don't let the perfect drive out the good." Some technologists look to the latest innovation and move directly to hardware and software decisions. The archival manager must insist that the team look at what is commercially available that meets the customer or staff needs. Waiting for the next advancement in software can prevent the timely acquisition of a needed system. Also, managers should insist that any system under serious consideration be tried on a prototype or pilot basis. When users are convinced that the proposed solution will work, enthusiasm and acceptance will build quickly. The information technology partnership can be a "win" for archival manager, staff, and customers.

Suggested Readings

The International Council of Archives' Committee on Archival Automation has produced an excellent, brief (twelve pages) overview entitled *Planning for Information Technology in Archives* (1996), which explains in lay language seven planning and decision-making processes and contains a useful list of resources. Also, G. Edward Evans, et al., *Management Basics for Information Professionals* has a chapter on "Managing Technology" (chapter 16) which includes a good overview of planning for information technology applications, uses of the Internet and intranet, and the critical need for staff training.

So much is being written on information technology that the best advice may be to use the Internet and review the past several years of *Records Management Quarterly,* the *American Archivist,* and the *Information Management Journal* for articles relevant to the archival manager's situation.

Chapter 8

Human Resources: The Critical Element

Besides leadership, managing human resources is the most critical topic discussed in this manual. The two are inextricably linked and at the heart of organizational success or failure. This chapter focuses on the difficult and critical task of managing people—every organization's most expensive and important asset. It is not about the formal operations of the human resources department. Rather, the focus is on the skills and knowledge needed by the archival manager to carry out human resources' responsibilities within the manager's program area, the archives. Obviously, this involves interaction with the human resources department as the manager often needs the expertise of personnel specialists to deal with employee-related issues.

People: The Central Resource

By now it should be clear that management is at least as much art or craft as science. Mary Parker Follett clearly understood the key test that managers face when she wrote, "management is the art of getting things done through people."[1] This is the acid test for managers

---

* Concepts for this section are drawn in part from a paper delivered by Daria D'Arienzo at the 1998 SAA meeting entitled "Making the Best Match: Setting the Context for Successful Staffing Decisions."

1 G. Edward Evans, Patricia Layzell Ward, and Bendik Rugaas, *Management Basics for Information Professionals* (New York and London: Neal-Schuman Publishers, Inc., 2000), 5.

because in no other area does the manager have to confront more directly the realities of what kind of person he or she is than when dealing with other people. No amount of managerial training can change the naturally shy, aloof person into an outgoing friendly one. Moreover, there are compelling reasons—practical as well as ethical—to argue that no management training program has the right to try. Ultimately, schemes that attempt to impose changes in attitude, behavior, and even personality on managers are less likely to be successful than those that aim for the less ambitious goal of helping managers identify their inclinations and interests. Self-awareness is almost certainly more important than adapting to a preconceived model.

Human resources management, at least on the scale likely to be practiced by most archival managers, involves direct and potentially uncomfortable contact with other people. These contacts can be frustrating and even painful; they can also be exciting and rewarding. Success in these dealings can be critical to the success of the organization for which a manager has accepted responsibility. How management treats people can define the whole character of an organization. No manager can afford to be indifferent to the task of directing the human resource. It means, ultimately, the difference between success and failure for every manager. Remembering that the staff is the central resource of the unit will keep the manager firmly focused on properly managing the most valuable asset available, the people in the organization.

Staff Partners

Knowledge-based organizations, perhaps more than other types, require collaborative, team-based operations to get the maximum input and benefit from all staff members. Archives, libraries, museums, and historical societies are certainly no exception. From the budget perspective, the greatest expenses are the salary and benefits for staff. Personnel costs, along with fixed facility expenses, usually dominate most organizations' budgets, often leaving little else available for other needs. So, from every management perspective, the type, quality, and adaptability of staff are crucial for organizational success. Managers are confronted with the question of what it means to form an organizationwide partnership with staff. An initial issue to confront is the type of staff needed. For long-established archival units this means taking an inventory of current staff competencies and looking ahead to future skills required by new programs or evolving technology. This would involve new recruiting strategies and quite possibly new strategies to retain those with marketable skills needed by the organization.

Newly established programs have the opportunity to build from the beginning the type of staff suitable to the organization's mission and operational needs. For those in small or single-person archives, the luxury of recruiting new staff is usually not an option. Archivists in these units must acquire new skills themselves to adjust to external and internal environmental change. Given the high cost of personnel, managers must also consider what mix of permanent and temporary staff is fiscally sustainable and properly balanced to meet mission goals and objectives. Many archival programs use grants as means of identifying project and program needs that can be addressed with defined, time-limited, temporary staff. Archives located near university archival education programs can often use interns to perform projects or reference activities that meet organizational needs and academic requirements.

Another option to consider is outsourcing. Never a favorite organizational option, it is sometimes a necessary one. Regardless of the size of the archival program, certain functions such as support services (e.g., printing, conservation) may be best performed by other parts of the parent institution or by external sources. The budget may not permit hiring staff on a permanent or long-term basis for certain tasks, yet these tasks must be performed. Outsourcing, while usually not inexpensive, does hold down long-term salary and benefits costs. Also, certain skills (e.g., information technology, project management) might be required only intermittently or cannot realistically be obtained through staff recruitment.

It is increasingly likely that the manager will have to form a team from permanent and temporary staff, interns, volunteers, and contractors. The manager must carefully identify what is actually needed for staffing the archives' programs and services. Determining the mix will often be a combination of trial and error and what financial resources are available. Certainly the manager must be clear about which tasks and functions are absolutely critical and which must be deferred no matter how distressing this may be for the manager, the institution, and stakeholder groups.

The leadership element in management comes to the fore at this point. The manager must be able to clearly articulate the vision for the program to staff (broadly defined above), the parent organization, and a host of external sources. Complementary to communicating vision, the manager must be able to motivate a staff made up of members with varied backgrounds and a varied expected length of tenure with the organization. From this mix, no matter how large or small, the manager must form a team and develop strategies to achieve institutional goals. Broadly speaking, if the manager cannot form a strong, cohesive team focused on achieving the mission, the program, at best, will fall short of success. The staff is the single greatest resource in the archival program. Therefore, getting staff members with the requisite knowledge and skills and keeping them motivated is key to success. Staff must not only be kept informed but should be brought into decision making as much as possible. Staff members usually know the work best, understand the demands of customers, and always share ideas on how to make things work better.

The manager should listen, assist the staff in trying to apply solutions to problems, and represent the staff to others in the organization. This last point is particularly important. If staff members are brought together to function in a fully collaborative manner as a team, they have certain expectations of the manager. The manager is not only the boss but an advocate: an advocate with upper management in the parent organization and with those outside the organization, and an advocate for additional resources, for operational flexibility, and for opportunities to develop as a team and individually. If the manager is perceived as an honest and effective advocate, staff members will understand that all that they seek is not obtainable. If the manager fails in this role, then staff disillusionment and turnover can be expected—a very costly outcome for the organization and the manager.

New Paradigm

The management paradigm presented throughout this manual is the complexity of contemporary organizational relationships. The relationship between the archival manager and the staff is a key element in these complexities. Part of this complexity is rooted in broad social, economic, and cultural changes affecting the workplaces of the twenty-first century. Information technology, for example, dramatically changes how services are provided to customers and how work is performed and managed. The family demands of working parents increasingly affect personnel policies and practices. Regardless of institutional setting, a variety of federal, state, and local laws and regulations affect every aspect of managing human resources. Civil rights and equal employment statutes, for example, require fair and objective, nondiscriminating processes for each stage in the manager-employee relationship—from the initial creation of the job through hiring, selection, and treatment on the job. From the economic perspective, mergers, downsizing, and outsourcing affect organizations and employees in profound ways.

From the perspective of organizing and managing work, the archival manager is often in the midst of a complex transition. Traditionally, work was viewed from the perspective of the industrial, assembly-line mode of operation. Jobs were broken down into component tasks and then assigned to an employee specifically recruited to perform that task. The demands of competitiveness, cost, and quality affect organizations in all sectors of the economy and are radically changing how work is organized and performed. This is leading to organizational relationships that are collaborative and group based. (See chapters 3 and 4 for further discussion.) Work-related tasks, many of which were previously the sole domain of management, are now performed in this new environment. Work groups, teams (ad hoc, recurring, cross-functional), communities of practice, hot groups, and other such phenomena increasingly dominate the workplace. Organizational complexity often requires the archival manager and staff to work on cross-functional teams involving not only the archival operation but other parts of the institution.[2]

---

2 For further discussion on this point see Marshall Sashkin and Molly G. Sashkin, *The New Teamwork: Developing and Using Cross-Function Teams* (New York: American Management Association, 1994).

Societal and organizational complexity are directly affecting policies and practices in the human resources management arena. Today's archival manager has a variety of tools not available to prior generations of managers. Jobs, whether performed by an individual employee or by those working in a group setting, can be executed in a variety of ways. Jobs can be shared between two individuals, which can meet the needs of the organization and staff members. The use of part-time employees, volunteers, and interns is increasingly coming to the fore (discussed elsewhere in this chapter). Information technology and organizational flexibility make possible telecommuting (sometimes referred to as teleworking or flexiplace). Employees can work part of their regular schedule from home, linked to the office via computer, fax machine, and telephone. Employees use adjusted work hours as another personnel strategy to build up credit time that can be taken later in lieu of vacation or sick leave.

Managing staff in such organizational complexity is both a challenge and an opportunity. A challenge because the gradual erosion of the command-and-control structure places new demands on the manager to ensure organizational effectiveness and productivity. Most of all, this involves mastering the subtleties of group dynamics and performance. But the personnel tools and strategies just described also provide a great opportunity. Meeting staff needs for greater control over their schedules and getting employees to buy in on organizing and performing work can reduce stress for managers and staff alike, improve morale, and boost productivity. Because so many archival organizations and parent institutions are in the midst of complex organizational change, the next three sections on recruitment, performance, and training and development will provide information and examples pertinent to traditional operations and those that are group- or team-based.

Recruitment

For program managers, recruitment is the first step in what will be an ongoing relationship with their staff member. Management expert Peter Drucker captured the importance of successful recruitment and selection of staff when he wrote, "People decisions are the ultimate—perhaps the only—control of an organization. People determine the performance capacity of an organization. No organization can do better than the people it has."[3] The recruitment—whether for a new position or to fill a vacancy—is the time to review what is really needed to meet the goals of the archives' program and the parent institution, if appropriate. Whether the program is small, medium, or large, the recruitment stage provides the opportunity to evaluate it in its entirety. The recruitment process involves several basic steps:

1. Recruitment Planning: The manager needs to review the mission and vision statements and the long- and short-range goals of the institution and the archives. This assists in determining job requirements and whether structural or other organizational changes must take place. From this review comes the traditional position description and job announcement (see figures 8-1 and 8-2), with the emphasis on the individual's position in the organization and his or her specific tasks and duties.

   In a team-based environment, the emphasis is on the collective nature of the tasks and the mutual responsibility for meeting organizational goals. (See figure 8-3.) Tasks formerly the exclusive domain of management are integrated into the team's operational purview, along with those involved in specific work processes.

   In all cases, duties must be clearly spelled out and specific knowledge, skills, and abilities identified in both position descriptions and job announcements.
2. Recruitment and Selection: Whether a traditional or team recruitment is undertaken, the position announcement needs to be advertised both within the institution and externally. When the recruitment is seeking external candidates, advertisements should be placed, either in print or on-line, in the SAA's job bulletin, regional archival publications, and the local

3 Peter F. Drucker, *Managing the Non Profit Organization: Principles and Practices* (New York: Harper Collins Publishers, 1990), 145.

Figure 8-1 Job Description

Job descriptions and job advertisements will differ in format and purpose; nonetheless, they must both present an accurate description of the position's essential responsibilities.

Society of American Archivists Education Director
(This is an abbreviated version.)

Key duties:

1. Leadership. Guide the education program to meet critical and challenging continuing education issues.
2. Advocacy. Assume leadership role in coordinating continuing education offerings provided by SAA and other education providers.
   - Liaison to other education providers
   - Coordinate with National Forum on Archival Continuing Education, Council of State Historical Records Coordinators, American Association for State and Local History.
3. Publishing. Develop and maintain course materials in a range of formats.
   - Work with SAA's Director of Publications to expand and market SAA's publications catalog.
4. Teaching. Develop and teach workshops and support other education providers in workshop design and development.

(Courtesy of the Society of American Archivists)

Figure 8-2 Job Advertisement

(This is an abbreviated version.)

Education Director
SAA is seeking a continuing education expert to serve as SAA's Education Director. The Education Director is responsible for guiding SAA's educational program; assuming a leadership role in coordinating continuing education offerings offered by SAA and serving as a liaison with other education providers; develops and publishes course materials in a wide range of formats; and develops and teaches workshops enabling archival experts to prepare traditional subject areas for new media presentation. This is a permanent, full-time position in the Society's Chicago office. Salary range is $40–$50K, with benefits. Minimum qualification of bachelor's degree in adult learning, five years relevant experience. Association management experience preferred. Send cover letter and resume to:

Executive Director
Society of American Archivists
527 S. Wells Street
5th Floor
Chicago, IL 60607

Fax 312-347-1452
info@archivists.org

No phone calls please.

(Courtesy of the Society of American Archivists)

Figure 8-3 Excerpt from Team Position Description

Nature and Complexity of the Work

The Maps and Plans Work Group is a multi-function team with responsibility for performing all archival functions on cartographic and architectural holdings. In addition, the work group team shares responsibility (with the Aerial Team) for providing on-site reference service for both media in the Cartographic Research Room. Archivists, technicians, and specialists jointly have taken control of, and are accountable for, the work that is performed by the team. Team members work together, each adding their own knowledge and expertise to help the team achieve its goals. Successful teams employ the knowledge, skills, and abilities of each member to their best use, and that takes an acquired ability and maturity of a relatively high level. Teams accept the responsibility for providing input for the annual operating plan, developing plans to achieve those goals, implementing the plans, and monitoring progress toward the goals. In addition, the work group assumes more of the responsibility for statistical reporting, managing work performance, assisting in the personnel selection process, and resolving contentious issues involving work and staff/team related issues.

By accepting the team concept as a way of performing work, the team members have assumed responsibility for all aspects of the work. It takes a good deal of effort, initiative, creativity, and just plain hard work to make the team function properly. This new aspect of the "work" they are asked to perform is in addition to their other, more traditional archival duties, adding to the difficulty and complexity of the job. In addition to the basic archival knowledge required, there is an additional body of technical, media, and historical knowledge that is required of members of the work group. The higher grade levels suggested in the proposed staffing pattern reflect these requirements, as well as reorganizing the fundamental change in the environment in which the work is performed.

(Courtesy of the National Archives and Records Administration)

media. Without a strong pool of candidates, the recruitment effort will come to naught.

The archival manager (and the team where appropriate) and the human resources specialist will review all applications based on the requirements in the job announcement to identify highly qualified candidates for interviews. The application review step includes developing a ranking or crediting strategy that uses the knowledge, skills, and abilities advertised in the job announcement and assigns points based on relevant education, training, or experience to identify the highly qualified. Considering aptitude demonstrated in work-related behavior, such as attitudes toward change and managing stress, is relevant and should be used in forming the pool of highly qualified candidates.

The interview is perhaps the most difficult and critical part of the entire process. Interviews must be carefully planned. EEO requirements and basic ethics require that all applicants should undergo a fair and critically objective evaluation. Appropriate questions should be prepared (see figure 8-4), and all applicants should be asked the same questions. The interview team should consist of the manager, team leaders or members if appropriate, and a human resources specialist. The interview process should include a tour of the facility and the opportunity for the applicant to meet with the human resources specialist to discuss compensation, benefits, and general working conditions. A key part of the process is a careful check of all references provided by the applicant of current and former employers. Checking with former employers can be particularly useful in getting an unfettered perspective. Make sure that there is documentation for all interviews and reference checks.

3. Orientation: The effectiveness of employee orientation directly affects the employee's long-term chances for success in the organization. Before commencing work, the employee should receive a copy of the position description, the organization's long-range or strategic plan, information about the employee's work unit or team, and human resources documentation, which needs to be completed prior to start date. The first days on the

Figure 8-4 Brief Guide to Legal Interview Questions

Topic	Legal Questions	Discriminatory Questions
Family Status	Do you have any responsibilities that conflict with job attendance or travel requirements?	Are you married? What is your spouse's name? What is your maiden name? Do you have any children? Are you pregnant? What are your childcare arrangements?
Race, Physical Characteristics	None	What is your race? Are you of Asian extraction? To what race do you belong? You're from Mexico, aren't you? Are you related to the Smith-Jones from Texas? (or similar, questions about descendants and parentage and questions about nationality of parents and spouse)
Religion	None (You may inquire about availability for weekend work.)	What is your religion? Which church do you attend? What are your religious holidays? Are you Catholic? What religious holidays will you be taking off if we hire you?

(continued)

Figure 8-4 continued

Topic	Legal Questions	Discriminatory Questions
Residence, Birthplace	What is your address? Where do you live? How long have you live in ______?	Do you own or rent your home? Who resides with you? Where were you born? Where were your parents born? May I see you birth certificate (or similar papers)?
Sex, Living Arrangements	None	Are you male or female? How many children do you have? Are you married?
Age	If hired, can you offer proof that you are at least 18 years of age?	How old are you? What is your birth date?
Arrests or Convictions of a Crime	Have you ever been convicted of a crime? (You must state that a conviction will be considered only as it relates to fitness to perform the job being sought.)	Have you ever been arrested?
Citizenship or Nationality	Can you show proof of your eligibility to work in the u.s.? Are you fluent in any languages other than English? (You may ask the second question only as it relates to the job being sought.)	Are you a u.s. citizen? Where were you born? Does your visa allow you to work?

(continued)

Figure 8-4 continued

Topic	Legal Questions	Discriminatory Questions
Disability, Physical Abilities or Limitations	The job requires lifting and carrying: can you do that? Are you able to perform the essential functions of this job without reasonable accommodation? (Show the applicant the position description so he or she can give an informed answer.)	Are you disabled? What is the nature or severity of your disability?
References	Statement that employment references will be checked.	Requirements for submission of "character" or religious references. ("Character" reference may be requested of security applicants.)
Notify in Case of Emergency	Name and address of person to be notified in case of accident or emergency.	Name and address of *relative* to be notified in case of accident or emergency.

("Brief Guide to Legal Interview Questions," by G. Edward Evans, Patricia Layzell Ward, and Bendik Rugaas, was reprinted from Management Basics for Information Professionals *with permission of the publisher. Copyright © 2000 by Neal-Schuman Publishers, Inc.)*

job should include a thorough review of all human resources rights, benefits, and responsibilities, as well as work requirements. Serious consideration should be given to using mentors to assist new employees in learning the organizational culture and "how we do things here." A bad start is difficult to correct and a good one can cope with problems that inevitably crop up.

Performance

In the workforce transition underway, performance evaluation systems will need to take into account employees executing assigned tasks in the traditional manner, those working in teams, and those working in a mixed environment. Whatever the situation, management and employee performance is essential to the success of the archival program. A key responsibility of management is to ensure successful employee performance.

Two basic areas should be considered in performance evaluation: workplace behavior (conduct) and job performance. The archival manager needs to be informed and understand the organization's standards for on-the-job conduct. If, in fact, workplace behavior standards are not in place, they must be developed with the assistance of human resources specialists. It is important to train all staff members on what is acceptable and unacceptable behavior in the workplace. It is a primary responsibility of management to ensure that the workplace is free from all forms of discriminatory behavior. The same behavior standards should be applicable to all employees. Archival managers should be sensitive to cultural traditions and expressions that have become an ever-increasing reality in a diverse workforce. Cultural differences are not necessarily indicators of either on-the-job conduct or performance ability.

Once behavior standards are in place, all employees should receive training on what is expected and how to respond to various workplace situations and problems. Archival managers should seek assistance from the human resources unit in providing this type of training. Often, outside vendors and consultants are able to provide needed expertise and experience that might not be available in-house.

Outside support may involve communication and listening skills, conflict management, supervisory skills, and assertiveness training.

In developing work performance standards, the basic competencies, knowledge, skills, and abilities identified in individual or team position descriptions form the basis for the standards. Whether performance standards are for individual employee or team goals and performance, measurements must be clearly identified. All goals relate to the organization's mission-critical tasks, and the standards combine both quantity and quality requirements. Also, performance measures must be developed to ensure fair employee performance evaluations. (See figure 8-5.) Archival managers should actively engage employees and teams in developing goals, standards, and measurements. This "buy-in" is needed to foster a sense of ownership on the part of everyone involved in the process. As performance standards are being developed, training or education needs must be identified so that employees and teams will have the opportunity and ability to achieve performance success. For teams, it is often useful to develop a charter that spells out the purpose, goals, and authority of the team. (See figure 8-6.) Management and team members should work together to prepare the charter, which forms part of the basis for establishing a team's performance plan and measuring its success.

Performance evaluations can often pose difficulties for both employees and managers. The manager should seek the employee's input on performance over the rating period and his or her goals for the next performance plan. In a teaming environment, all team members should review the team's performance and each team member's contribution to that performance. One technique increasingly used in the corporate sector, primarily though not exclusively for managers, is called "360° feedback." This involves "collecting perceptions about a person's behavior and the impact of that behavior from the person's boss or bosses, direct reports, colleagues, fellow members of project teams, internal and external customers, and suppliers."[4]

After seeking input from individual employees or team members, it is the manager's responsibility to make the final determination and then

4 Richard Lepsinger and Antoinette D. Lucia, *360° Feedback* (San Francisco: Jossey-Bass Pfeiffer, 1997), 6.

Figure 8-5 Performance Effectiveness Management Systems

Mission Critical Areas	Quality Standards	Performance Measures
Reference Service	40 percent of users will assess the quality of reference and info services as excellent on a scale of one to five (five = excellent)	a. Satisfaction with service b. Number of customers served c. Cost of providing Reference Service
Library Instruction	90 percent of workshop participants will be satisfied with instruction received as measured by an evaluation at the end of the workshop	a. Number of quick fact and bibliographical questions b. Accuracy of reference and staff responses c. Customer satisfaction with reference service
Customer Responsiveness	95 percent of complaints received will be responded to within two working days and judged as "satisfactory responses" by 90 percent of those submitting the request	a. Satisfaction with response b. Complaint response time c. Number of complaints received
Financial Reporting and Monitoring	60 percent of interlibrary loan books requested will be available for checkout within fourteen days of request	a. Cycle time of book borrowing process b. Number of books requested c. Cost of book request process d. Customer satisfaction with turn-around time

(Reproduced by permission of the American Library Association from "Using Performance Measurement to Evaluate Teams and Organizational Effectiveness" [Carrie Russell, Library Administration and Management, *vol. 12, no. 3, p. 162]; copyright 1998 by the American Library Association.)*

Figure 8-6 Sample Team Charter

Team	National Archives Experience Core Team
Purpose	To manage the National Archives Experience project
Goals	To develop and implement a concept for exhibits and education at the National Archives (on the Mall, in cyberspace, and on the road) that exceeds the expectations of visitors, responds to NARA's strategic plan and inspires the support of the Foundation for the National Archives.
Strategic Plan Connection	Goal 2F of NARA Strategic Plan: "We will expand public access to documentation of the national experience by seeking public-private partnerships to fund a permanent exhibit around the Charters of Freedom as well as other new exhibits with associated educational materials that we can circulate physically, electronically, or both."
Duration	About 3 years — or until we are ready to open.
Participating NW Unit(s)	Museum Programs unit (as core team)
Other Participating NARA Offices	Work closely with the Archivist and other program staff as the project evolves
Accountability Point	Museum programs unit

(continued)

Figure 8-6 continued

Program Lead(s)[i]	N/A
Supervisory Manager(s)[ii]	Marvin Pinkert
Team Leader(s)[iii]	Chris Smith, Lee Ann Potter
Team Members	Pinkert, Smith, Potter, M.L. Jackson, Ruskin, Bustard; and as time permits Bredhoff
Tasks/Products & Milestones	Concept Presentation—October 21, 2001 Finished Design Concept—January 15, 2002 Final Design and Scripts—September, 2002 Contracts with Fabricators—May, 2003 Exhibit Installed—May, 2004 Exhibit Opened—July, 2004
Additional Resources Needs[iv]	Team relies on external and professional expertise; most pressing needs are in the area of providing consultation to the Foundation on contract development.
Training Needs[v]	Use of project management tools
Communication Methods	Mainly e-mail and regular meetings

i Program Lead(s): Organizational unit with primary responsibility for the team or work group.
ii Supervisory Manager(s): Supervisor of the team or work group.
iii Team Leader(s): Person(s) responsible for day-to-day work of the team or work group.
iv Additional Resource Needs: May include supplies, equipment, funding.
v Training Needs: May include training in the handling of administrative topics, management, work skills, interpersonal communication, teamwork, consensus building, or performance measurement.

(continued)

Figure 8-6 continued

Basic Team Ground Rules[vi]	Mutual respect. Willingness to say what's on our minds and to listen to the opinions of others. We do not make decisions on the basis of compromise and consensus, but rather by reasoned advocacy and adherence to our goals.
Reporting Mechanisms	Weekly meetings with the Archivist, biweekly reports to the Assistant Archivist
Plan Review Date	January 15, 2002 — estimated date of completion for concept phase

vi Basic Team Ground Rules: Various statements as to how the team will operate in such arenas as assigning projects, decision making, manager/staff expectation and communication, identifying and solving problems, and individual responsibilities to team, interaction with other team members, conflict resolution, adequacy of performance, and other teaming dynamics.

(Courtesy of the National Archives and Records Administration)

discuss the results with the employees. The manager should prepare a written evaluation in advance of the meeting. The manager should be low-key and objective in discussing the employee's strengths and weaknesses, and the rationale for the final rating. The employee should be allowed to respond at that point or after some time is provided for employee review and consideration. In most circumstances, the emphasis should be on what is expected in the coming year and the identification of strategies and resources needed to strengthen performance.

An integral part of evaluation performance is reward and recognition. Traditionally, recognition for good performance has come in the form of cash bonuses, promotions, or within-grade increases. Monetary rewards, of course, should remain as one method of recognition, but there are other approaches. Money is not always the primary motivation for staff or managers. Recognition for excellent performance can be done through awards ceremonies (using medals or plaques), articles in newsletters about accomplishments, time off from work scheduled at the employee's convenience, or opportunities for further professional development. The reward and recognition system should reflect differing levels and types of achievement. A timely recognition ("spot award") for contributing to a particular event, for example, could be a ballpoint pen or some other item for the desk. The system utilized should be clear, in writing, and part of personnel policies and practices.

Helping Employees Succeed

Most managers find personnel problems to be the most difficult they must face. Leaky roofs and inadequate budgets are one thing; dealing with a poorly performing or disgruntled employee is something else entirely. Most repository staffs are small in size, and the employee whose performance is in question may well be a longtime colleague or friend, making the situation even more difficult. How should the manager proceed?

Deficient performance can result from a number of causes. Is the employee capable of doing the assigned job? Are the tools—including training—sufficiently provided to the employee to permit a job's successful completion? Are the duties set forth in the job description realistic, both in the amount and level of work required of the employee? Before assuming that an employee is failing because of his or her inadequacies, management needs to make sure that it is not assisting failure or making it inevitable. Has some circumstance, internal or external, rendered the employee's job description out of date? Suppose management has implemented a successful outreach program that, over a short period of time, doubles the number of researchers using a repository. Has the increase in the number of researchers using the repository made it impossible for the reference staff to perform its functions? Has the decision to accept a valuable but deteriorating collection forced a preservation staff member to put aside routine or previously scheduled work?

Once the problem has been identified, the manager must devise a remedy. Is training available to correct deficiencies? Can other personnel be assigned, even part time, to assist an overburdened colleague, at least until it can be determined that the increased workload is not an aberration?

If the manager determines that the problem lies with the employee, he or she should arrange to discuss it with that person. This can be an uncomfortable step for both manager and employee, but several guidelines may help:

1. Focus on performance, not personality.
2. Within reason, recognize that doing things differently is not the same as doing things poorly.
3. Reserve judgment until the employee has had a chance to explain his or her view of the situation.
4. Invite the employee to suggest ways to rectify the situation.
5. In both word and behavior, emphasize a preference for encouraging success, not noting failure.

The last point is critical. Employees' reactions to counseling may depend far more on how they think the manager feels about them than on the specific issues discussed. Is the manager out to encourage employees to do better? Or is the emphasis on restating who's in charge? Is the manager willing to listen to what an employee has to say? Or has the manager already reached a judgment on the matter under discussion? This is not a choice between being a nice person and being an effective manager. No manager can guarantee that employees will approve of every management decision. Managers can enhance the likelihood that employees will respect those decisions by creating a work environment in which mutual respect for all members of the staff is encouraged, along with a dedication to achieving common goals.

What about the possibility of personal problems? Generally, these are of no concern to the manager, unless work is disturbed through chronic absence or lateness, lengthy phone conversations at the worksite, or the employee's inability to put aside personal problems on the job. Accepting a management position does not, however, involve resigning from the human race. Managers should be sympathetic to an employee undergoing personal stress. Deaths of loved ones, illness in the family, and personal disappointments happen to everyone. Moreover, even in the most bureaucratic situations, people establish personal contacts and relationships with their coworkers, including their bosses. Managers must be realistic in assessing the degree to which subordinates will bring their personal lives into the workplace, and they must be equally realistic in expecting that even the most conscientious employee will encounter periods of reduced effectiveness. Managers must also recognize that their subordinates are also colleagues (and even friends), and they should not be unwilling to react to them in those capacities.

At some point, however, the manager may need to counsel an employee whose performance has declined, perhaps as the result of personal problems. The manager may even suggest that the employee consider seeking assistance from personal or social service providers available either within the organization or from the community at large. Human resources offices in large organizations should be equipped either to provide services or to make a wide range of referrals.

Managers need to keep in mind the limits of both their authority and their capabilities in counseling employees. Every large organization has its share of office therapists, but this role needs to be approached carefully. The manager who crosses beyond clearly determined limits in performing such functions runs the risk of seeing his or her own effectiveness reduced and perhaps even of making a difficult situation worse.

Effective managers create a climate in which members of an organization share a sense of contribution and participation in the organization's mission. In such a climate, most discipline should be the self-discipline of people sharing in a cooperative effort, under conditions and practices they see as conducive to that effort. This objective is most likely to be met where communication on goals and procedures is encouraged and where employees feel free to participate in their development. W. Edward Deming, one of the foremost management consultants of the postwar era, has written that performance evaluations and annual ratings are among the "seven deadly sins" committed by managers and organizations.[5] Managers who find themselves spending much of their time *solving* problems with employees should consider whether they have put enough emphasis on *preventing* problems.

Understandably, managers can spend a great deal of time with employees who have difficulties. But the manager also has a responsibility to help those employees who are doing well. This involves building a relationship between the manager and staff member focused on how good performance can be improved for greater organizational effectiveness and individual growth and satisfaction. The manager and staff can also identify areas in which the manager needs to improve. One tool that can be used in helping staff and manager alike is the individual development plan (IDP). The IDP is not part of the formal evaluation process, but is used to identify those skills, abilities, and job-related experience that the staff member seeks to enhance and improve. The IDP is a tool that organizational development specialists can use to assist the manager in developing the staff.

Training and Development

If people are an organization's most important resource, it follows that they should be treated with due regard for the human potential for change and growth. Every organization, no matter how small, needs a program for staff development—even if the staff consists only of one archivist. Employee development programs can encompass extensive training efforts, conferences, and seminars. But they can begin simply, with a statement from the organization of its policies toward employee development. Will the organization reimburse employees for training or membership in professional organizations? At a minimum, can the institution's budget permit employees to be paid while they attend professional meetings? Does the organization provide access to professional literature? Is information on meetings and workshops run by SAA, regional organizations, or by the parent

5 G. Edward Evans, Patricia Layzell Ward, and Bendik Rugaas, *Management Basics for Information Professionals* (New York and London: Neal-Schuman Publishers, Inc., 2000), 410.

institution posted or otherwise brought to the attention of staff members?

Limited resources can determine the shape and extent of a career development program; they should not be excuses for their absence. Many workshops and conferences are available at nominal cost, and employees should expect to shoulder at least part of the burden for education and other opportunities of which they, as much as their employers, are the beneficiary. In some cases, an organization's only support to employees seeking an advanced degree or other training may be time off the job to attend class. The benefits of career development should be especially attractive to archival institutions, which invest heavily in skills developed only after long experience with a collection, its donors, and its researchers. Employee turnover will occur under the best of circumstances, but for an archives to lose personnel because a job has been outgrown and management has made no plans for career development can be especially painful. While an employee may be replaced with someone with equivalent or even superior credentials, the institution will still have suffered a loss.

Career development efforts need to be geared to the varying career levels of employees. Clerical and technical personnel may be interested in developmental opportunities in their fields, but they may also be interested in acquiring the credentials necessary for professional status. Professionals, especially those with advanced degrees, place extremely high value on independence, and development programs need to reflect this. Sabbaticals or programs permitting interested staff members time off for writing or research are valuable both to the institution and to the profession as a whole. Institutions have an obligation, within resource limits, to encourage staff members to participate actively in the meetings and publications that are the center of any profession's being. Because the average archival institution is far removed from the size and breadth of Fortune 500 companies, opportunities for promotion, not to mention significant monetary remuneration, for archivists can be limited. Archival managers can, realistically, do little to change this. They can, however, encourage the growth of skills and experience that will enhance the archivist's sense of participation and contribution in his or her chosen field.

Volunteers and Interns

Most archival institutions depend to one degree or another on adjunct employees, whether interns or volunteers. These can be extremely valuable staff members, stretching the limited resources available to most repositories. In many respects, adjunct interns should be managed like other members of the staff, with appropriate attention paid to those areas in which they are not like other members of the staff. These boil down, largely, to terms of employment and hours. Interns generally will be with the repository for a brief, fixed period of time. Though volunteers may be "on board" for a longer period, they are surely not there under the same status as permanent, paid staff members.

These considerations determine, to a large extent, the management of adjunct personnel. How much training is a manager willing to give an intern who will only be available for a few months? How much responsibility should be entrusted to a volunteer who is only available on an irregular basis? Managers need to ensure that volunteers and interns result in a "profit" to the institution; that is, that the investment in their training does not exceed the benefit the institution derives from their presence. In dealing with interns, managers need to ensure that the terms of the internship, as agreed upon with the sponsoring school or other institution, are followed. If the internship will result in course credit or some other benefit, the intern's performance needs to be monitored so that the institution can attest to the completion of the internship.

While volunteers can be a wonderful resource, they can also test a manager's skill. Volunteers gain a measure of independence from their status that only a foolish manager would overlook. While recognizing that volunteers may be exempt from some rules that apply to the permanent staff, management needs to make clear which rules apply to all. For instance, volunteers should be expected to work the hours for which they are scheduled.

Conclusion

Managers are expected to master a variety of skills, roles, and tasks. But if a manager can excel in only one area, let it be in leading and managing people! Poor management of human resources is an absolute guarantee of failure. A motivated, informed, and well-led staff can compensate for a host of other organizational deficiencies and achieve truly outstanding results. Most archival managers have limited resources and time available for their own training. That being the case, managers should seek out workshops and seminars that help them understand themselves and their style of leadership as well as personality types and organizational and group behaviors. Planning, organizing, budgeting, project management, and the like can be learned over time through trial and error. Understanding human dynamics requires systematic, professional development that continues throughout a career.

Suggested Readings

Books and articles in the human resources management arena are too numerous to list. While the literature on human resources management in the archival field is limited, there are extensive sources in related fields of endeavor. *The Journal of Library Administration and Management,* for example, contains numerous useful articles, such as "Cross Functional Teams" by Bonnie A. Osif and Richard L. Harwood (vol. 2, no. 1, winter 1997); and "Using Performance Measurement to Evaluate Teams and Organizational Effectiveness" by Carrie Russell (vol. 12, no. 3, summer 1998). Another useful source is the *Bulletin of the American Society for Information Science.* G. Edward Evans, et al., in *Management Basics for Information Professionals* has a lengthy discussion on managing personnel (chapter 14) with a fairly comprehensive list of sources.

Chapter 9

Communication: The Critical Ingredient

This manual discusses a variety of management tasks requiring assorted skills and abilities. All these tasks—planning, budgeting, organizing, and leading people—depend on effective communication to succeed. So many people and organizations bemoan the lack of communication or its poor quality that it is almost a cliche to blame everything on "poor communication." Yet in many situations it truly is a fundamental problem.

What Is It?

Communication is something we do all day every day. It seems so normal we usually do not think about what is really happening. In point of fact, communication is a very complex phenomenon involving the senses, emotions, and logic. Experts such as linguists have long studied the two-way process called communication. Whenever communication occurs, either between individuals or in a group setting, there is such an abundance of sensory stimuli as well as emotional factors, sometimes labeled biases or blinders, that what is said or heard is only a highly condensed or abstract version. This creates obviously fertile ground for poor communication and trouble.

Several elements comprise communication: verbal, nonverbal, and listening. Words can be spoken or written and the communication expressed through words is more than the linear, progressive unfolding of logic. Words reflect cultural backgrounds, have different meanings in different contexts, and can be difficult to interpret if the words or thoughts are too abstract. Nonverbal messages (i.e., tone of voice, body language, and facial expressions), in fact, are estimated to account for more than 90 percent of communication between people, while verbal communication is estimated at 10 percent. Listening, a skill that can be supported and strengthened by training, is another critical element of communication. Sensory overload and feelings or emotions influence effective listening acutely and can affect what is heard or understood.

Communication Challenges

In discussing communication, we should realize that the prudent manager, in fact all involved in the communication process, should more often than not expect to be misunderstood. This observation is based on the complex nature of the communication process and the certainty that communication problems are endemic. The very elements of communication, verbal, nonverbal, and listening, contain the seeds of some very difficult problems. Words are problematic. What is straightforward and easily understood by one person has a totally different connotation for someone else. Racial, ethnic, and socio-economic factors influence the meaning of words. Furthermore, it is difficult to communicate abstract thoughts or emotions, for that matter, because words cannot express every aspect of meaning or feeling. Our minds are constantly seeking to understand new facts and situations and evaluate them in existing mental models. Words can actually be confusing rather than clarifying.

Even seemingly simple on-the-job communications can be fraught with difficulty. Memos, directives, and other written messages can appear to the author to be clear, objective expositions of facts and policies. Yet the words or concepts are often misunderstood by the recipients, who will read the items from their own perspective or context. This is where emotions or psychological factors come into the picture. Work assignments, leave policies, or disciplinary actions, for example, can be received with a variety of feelings and opinions, depending on the organization's culture and the psychological makeup or experiences of staff members. Multicultural differences can also affect the efficacy of written communication. Differing values, language structures, and meanings of words pose their own significant challenges. Nonverbal messages, as previously noted, are an extremely important element in communication. Within groups or between individuals, nonverbal messages can often tell the tale. Raised eyebrows, crossed arms or legs, facial grimaces, and vacant stares all indicate communication problems. Particularly in a supervisor-subordinate situation, nonverbal messages can clearly express what a staff member is really thinking or feeling. Nonverbal messages often contradict the spoken word.

Communication challenges occur in any hierarchical organization. Barriers to effective communication increase as the bureaucratic layers and controls increase. One of the advantages of teaming is that, by consolidating work processes and eliminating layers of management, communication can be simplified. Signs of organizational trouble invariably include communication issues such as negative nonverbal messages, a deterioration in information sharing, and verbal communication that consistently misses its intended purpose. All this indicates declining productivity and problematic mission achievement.

Yet, the inevitability of communication problems does not mean all is hopeless. Far from it. Good communication is like any other skill. It must be mastered and practiced over and over if performance is to improve. Perhaps the best place to start is with that element of communication that seems the easiest: listening.

Listening—The Communications Clue

While listening might seem the easiest and most natural element in communication, authors Ralph G. Nichols and Leonard A. Stevens put the issue in perspective: "The effectiveness of the spoken word hinges not so much on how people talk but mostly on how they listen."[1]

1 Ralph G. Nicholas and Leonard A. Stevens, "Listening to People," *Harvard Business Review on Communications* (Cambridge, Mass.: Harvard Business Review, Paperback, 1999), 1.

In the workplace, and particularly in management work, the spoken word is arguably more important than the written word. But we are trained to read and write, not to listen. In fact, it is difficult to retain what we hear. Within one work day (eight hours) we will forget 30 to 50 percent of what we heard in lectures, presentations, or conversation. Managers often rely on oral communication to get information up the chain of command, to direct subordinates, or to provide information to peers in the organization or to the public. Our difficulty in retaining what we hear, or even in understanding it in the first place, sets the stage for miscommunication and trouble.

Our minds work much faster than we can speak. (See figure 9-1.) So, as we are listening to someone there is "space" between what we are hearing and what we are thinking. In this "space" we might think ahead to what we will say, if we are in a conversation, or anticipate where a speaker might be going in a lecture. We might be evaluating and judging what we hear, trying to mentally figure out what the speaker has said, or listen between the lines to figure out what the speaker is "really" saying. In other words, the possibility of misunderstanding what we hear is very high; hence the phrase, "they were just talking past each other."

Just as we had to learn to read and write, we have to learn to listen. Active listening takes commitment and practice. We need to develop an open mind and withhold judgments until we have heard someone out. It is futile and counterproductive to be marshaling our arguments before we have heard and understood what someone is saying. Human emotions certainly come into play. Sometimes, certain individuals or issues trigger an almost instantaneous negative reaction. It takes a great deal of discipline and practice to keep an open mind and to listen for understanding. When listening, try to group the ideas being expressed and not to memorize each word. Look for the point, the big picture, the speaker is trying to communicate. Granted, some speakers, or colleagues, are better oral communicators than others. But we need to actively listen to the idea, issue, or problem being expressed. Failure to understand can cause grievous harm to the organization, particularly in times of crisis or when facts need to be accurately grasped and reported to others.

One can use certain strategies to improve active listening. To counter our emotional filters and mental biases, we can mentally

Figure 9-1 Communication Case Study

A, the boss is talking to B, the subordinate, about a new program that the firm is planning to launch. B is a poor listener. In this instance, he tries to listen well, but he has difficulty concentrating on what A has to say.

A starts talking and B launches into the listening process, grasping every word and phrase that comes into his ears. But right away B finds that, because of A's slow rate of speech, he has time to think of things other than the spoken line of thought. Subconsciously, B decides to sandwich a few thoughts of his own into the aural ones that are arriving so slowly. So B quickly dashes out into a mental sidetrack and thinks something like this: "Oh, yes, before I leave I want to tell A about the big success of the meeting I called yesterday." Then B comes back to A's spoken line of thought and listens for a few more words.

There is plenty of time for B to do just what he has done, dash away from what he hears and then return quickly, and he continues taking sidetracks to his own private thoughts. Indeed, he can hardly avoid doing this because over the years the process has become a strong aural habit of his.

But, sooner or later, on one of the mental sidetracks, B is almost sure to stay away too long. When he returns, A is moving along ahead of him. At this point it becomes harder for B to understand A, simply because B has missed part of the oral message. The private mental sidetracks become more inviting than ever, and B slides off onto several of them. Slowly he misses more and more of what A has to say.

When A is through talking, it is safe to say that B will have received and understood less than half of what was spoken to him.

(Courtesy of the Harvard Business Review, *found in* HBR on Effective Communication, *Nichols and Stevens, "Listening to People," 7–8)*

search out evidence presented by what the speaker said that counters our own attitudes and opinions. Assume the speaker is right and see if our point of view really holds up. If we have truly heard what is said, countered our biases, and re-examined our own opinions, we might indeed come to a different perspective—all from active listening. Other aspects of an active listening strategy include not interrupting someone who is speaking, keeping eye contact with the other person, and being sensitive to nonverbal messages. As noted previously, nonverbal messages can more accurately convey feelings and opinions than the spoken word. Also, particularly in dealing with staff members, the manager should be sensitive to the time and place of a conversation. Sensitive issues or problems require mindfulness on the part of the speaker and the listener.

If we approach listening with an open mind, a willingness to weigh evidence, and an awareness of our own biases, the possibilities of good communication will dramatically improve. But one office ritual, the meeting, can severely test our good intentions.

Meetings and Presentations

Some years ago, a management training video came out entitled *Meetings, Bloody Meetings!* Use of humor made the painful reality explored in the film bearable. Most people in most organizations regard most meetings as an utter waste of time and talent. Unfortunately, that is often the case. A manager known for poorly conceived, overly lengthy, and inconclusive meetings will ultimately drive the staff away or will find it rebellious and uncooperative. At that point, effective decision making and implementation are fatally undermined. Yet, meetings are an essential ingredient in work life. Humans are social beings. We need to belong, to communicate, to come together. From a practical perspective, the workplace is a complex arena, and information dissemination, decision making, and the work itself all require meetings. So, because meetings are essential and inevitable, it is critical how they are conceived, organized, and managed.

The first issue is what type of meeting? Is it designed to gather or disseminate information, to make decisions, or for team members working on a special project or work process? The purpose for meeting should help determine frequency and size. Information-gathering meetings are held on an as-needed basis and include everyone with relevant information to share. These are often predecisional meetings, though not all participants may be included in the decision-making meeting to follow. Information-disseminating meetings should also be held as needed and can have a significant number of attendees; including all those who need to understand a new policy, initiative, or workplace issue.

Decision-making or management meetings are usually held on a regular basis—weekly, biweekly, or monthly. Within an archives program, the manager and subordinate supervisors meet for policy discussions, while the manager participates in management meetings of the parent organization. These meetings have the overall purpose of setting goals, anticipating or resolving conflicts, and monitoring performance.

Certain basic elements are required for successful meetings. The manager must set the right tone. As with active listening, the manager must have an open mind and encourage ideas and participation. (See figure 9-2.) An agenda must be prepared and distributed before each meeting. The agenda helps identify the goals and purposes of the meeting. Time limits should be set for each agenda item to assist the leader to push the meeting along to a successful conclusion. Meetings should last one hour; two at most. After one to two hours, participants have great difficulty staying focused, and the meeting rapidly becomes dysfunctional. Careful preparation—ensuring that the right people attend the meeting, securing a meeting space conducive to effective communication, and distributing the agenda and any background materials in advance — paves the way for a successful meeting.

In running the meeting, the manager must be sensitive to hidden agendas and lack of candor on the part of participants. These are to be expected, particularly in hierarchical organizations with supervisor-subordinate dynamics in play. Regardless of the type of meeting, the manager must establish a climate that fosters a variety of ideas and points of view, even though not all ideas will be accepted. Ideas should be treated and explored in a respectful way by the entire group. The manager should seek to diminish competition, encourage the group to identify the strengths of the ideas presented, and explore how weaknesses

Figure 9-2 Contrasting the Assumptions of a Judgmental Manager and a Judicious Manager

Judgmental Manager	Judicious Manager
The most efficient mode is to have one boss call the shots.	The most efficient mode is to make use cooperatively of the varied talents available.
I must protect my power to make decisions.	The best decision will emerge if I combine my power with that of the implementers.
I decide every course of action where I am authorized to decide.	I enlist my subordinates to devise courses of action and contribute my thoughts as matters progress.
I must exercise all the autonomy my power permits.	I must use my power to help my subordinate develop his or her autonomy.
I use my power for my own growth.	I share my power so that my subordinates can grow as I grow.
I motivate people.	Accomplishment motivates people. I can provide opportunities for accomplishment.
I review, oversee, and control the efforts of my subordinates.	I use my experience, power, and skill to aid subordinates in accomplishing the task.
I take credit for the results of the groups I manage.	I explicitly recognize the accomplishments of subordinates.

(continued)

Figure 9-2 continued

Judgmental Manager	Judicious Manager
To get results I must spot flaws and have them corrected.	To get results we must help each other overcome flaws.
When subordinates express themselves or act in ways unacceptable to me, I point out the flaws.	When subordinates express themselves or act in unacceptable ways, I assume they had reasons that made sense to them and explore the action from that point of view.
As mature people we are able to "take" put-downs and criticism without destructive consequences.	Even mature people are distressed to some degree by put-downs and criticism, and this makes cooperation difficult.
My role is to define the mission of my group.	My role in mission definition is to facilitate discovery by my subordinates and myself.
My role is to make judgments about the actions of my subordinates while they are carrying out our mission.	My role is to join my subordinates to make sure they succeed.

(Courtesy of the Harvard Business Review, *found in* HBR on Effective Communication, *George M. Prince, "Creative Meetings Through Power Sharing," 71)*

can be overcome. Humor can soften criticism of ideas and keep the tone of the meeting constructive.

Meetings often involve making presentations. The manager may make a presentation at a staff meeting in his or her own unit, at a meeting elsewhere in the organization, or to an external audience. Regardless of the setting, the presenter should remember five critical success factors. (See figure 9-3.) Successfully carrying out these steps assures that other meeting participants know that they are the manager's focus. Good back and forth communication is likely to result.

Staff, Peers, the Boss

The manager is communicating every minute of every day on the job. Phone calls, conversations, e-mails, messages, and memos fill the day. It is vitally important to be clear about who is the audience for all this communication. Chapter 13 on public relations focuses on communication with external audiences. This section focuses on three critical internal audiences—staff, peers, and boss.

No matter how small or large the staff, the manager interacts with its members on a daily basis. It is important to continually communicate with the staff the shared values, mission, and goals of the archives and the parent institution. This can be done through hallway conversations and informal sessions or in more formal ways by team charters, performance plans and evaluations, program reviews, newsletters, or even videos for those with staff in dispersed locations. E-mail messages and e-mail banners are excellent ways to get information out very quickly. Communicating with the staff must be the result of a well–thought-out strategy. Size and composition of the staff, geographic location, and who needs to know what to get the job done must be taken into account. These considerations will influence the scheduling and frequency of meetings, the mix of oral and written communication, and even how to manage informal communication.

If the archives is large enough to have first-line supervisors, these individuals are really the key to communicating with the staff. Most employees get their information from their immediate supervisor. So,

Figure 9-3 Key Factors for Successful Presentations

CSF	Steps to Take
1. Don't waste time	• Be prepared with mastery of the topic • Leave time for questions and answers • Make sure equipment or slides, transparencies, PowerPoint, computer presentations, and all logistics are arranged
2. Know the audience	• Ensure that remarks are focused and specific • Handouts should be appropriate to points under discussion
3. Be organized	• Explain how the presentation is organized • Get to the point • Repeat main point two or three times • Keep material to a minimum
4. Be qualified	• Don't talk until you have mastered the subject • Have other experts present if needed • Communicate your expertise
5. Finish strongly	• Let attendees know when you are concluding • End with a strong reiteration of the main point • Use an anecdote or quote if appropriate • Make the concluding comment after the question-and-answer period is over.

(Adopted and modified from Karen Susman, "Six Key Indicators Guaranteed to Reduce Audience Stress and Increase Your Applause," Records Management Quarterly *[July 1997]: 18–22)*

it is critical that the first-line supervisor be kept informed, ahead of the staff, about major initiatives, projects, or new policies. The first-line supervisor should be the one to communicate face-to-face with employees about significant issues and events, always accurately conveying the facts of the situation.

Relations with management peers in the institution are always delicate. Here, the manager must also work out formal and informal strategies for communication. In formal management meetings, the archival manager should ensure that archives' issues, particularly those that affect other units, are put on the agenda on a regular basis. Informally, the manager should keep in contact with peers by "dropping in" for informal conversations and keeping in touch with phone calls or e-mail messages. The point is that the archives will always need support and assistance from other units. Clear communication between managers based on enlightened self-interest will help the archives in its day-to-day operations and hopefully will do likewise in times of crisis or opportunity.

Communication with the boss is also a sensitive issue. The manager must first ascertain how much the boss really wants to know and the manner in which the boss wishes to get information. This means the archivist must get to know the boss. If at first the boss isn't too interested, then the manager needs to learn, probably through trial and error, what will peak the boss's interest. Perhaps the boss is interested in public outreach activities, researchers, or acquisition. The manager should engage the boss in areas of interest and then paint a broader context of the archival operation as a whole. This can be done informally in conversations or by sending along items of interest. Formal settings include management meetings, program reviews, and performance plan sessions. Obviously, a mix of strategies must be employed to keep the archives' program visible and clearly relevant to the boss and the entire organization.

A final point must be made. All the strategies discussed in this section are useless if the manager is not perceived as a person of integrity whose communications can be relied upon to be truthful and accurate. If staff, peers, and boss do not trust what the manager has to say, communication ends before it begins. This signifies a truly dysfunctional situation. To avoid this, the manager must be clear, precise, and prudent in all communication to avoid getting tagged as an unreliable communicator.

Communication Tools

Any discussion about communications in the modern workplace must deal with the revolution in communications technology over the past two decades. Most organizations, including archives, have computers available for most if not all staff. These computers usually have, at a minimum, electronic mail, Internet, and Web capabilities. Based on these capabilities, many organizations have developed intranets (using data communication standards of the Internet and the Web), which can link people and information throughout the organization. An intranet can be an excellent tool for the manager to use within the archival unit. The electronic posting of policy documents, manuals, meeting notices, access to external databases, and other items, can contribute to organizational knowledge, assist in democratizing the workplace, and enhance productivity. The archival manager will need to work with the archives' or the parent institution's information technology staff to create an intranet capability or to make it more robust and useful for the archival program. While the problem of information overload is a real one, the intranet makes it easy to update and disseminate information. Also, teams, communities of practice, and hot groups all need this tool to flourish and thrive.

The archival manager must also understand the various capabilities and tools available on the Internet. Researching information about a collection or records creator, identifying additional sources of information for a researcher, or gathering data for administrative tasks involving finance or purchasing can all benefit from effective use of the Internet and the Web. Web browsers, software programs used to review sites on the Web, can retrieve text as well as support graphics, hyperlinks, sound, and images. Two of the more popular browsers are Netscape Navigator and NCSA Mosaic. Search strategies involve familiarity and use of Web search directories and search engines. Directories are designed like telephone books, with predefined categories that list topics that can be searched. Some of the more popular directories are Yahoo, Magellan, and Ultrasearch. More robust and flexible are search engines into which keywords or concepts are typed, databases are searched, and lists of documents or URLs (Internet addresses, or "Uniform Resource Locators") containing those terms are identified. Popular search engines include Alta Vista, Excite, Hotbot, Infoseek, and Lycos.

Communication Strategies

Because effective communication is so important to organizational success, the manager must develop coherent, well–thought-out strategies to manage not only the plethora of tools available but also the accompanying flood of information. These electronic communication tools—e-mail, the intranet, Web search directories and engines, PowerPoint presentations—could conceivably harm the unit if all the information involved is not managed from a strategic perspective.

The clarity and focus required for meetings and presentations have already been noted. Using computer graphics, PowerPoint, slides, or transparencies are only means to the end identified by the manager, as is the case with the intranet. Staff can be overwhelmed with a flood of information and access to numerous databases. What is the point? The manager must assess the information needs of the staff, the level of automated access available to the staff, and the sophistication of staff members in utilizing automated tools. Only those policies, procedures, or information (e.g., emergency preparedness plans) really needed by the staff should be put on the intranet. Administrative information and forms lend themselves to intranet access, but only what is needed by the staff should be made available. The intranet is not cost free. Information must be continually updated because if staff perceive the information is dated, use will plummet.

E-mail with attachments can speed the drafting and review of correspondence and reports, but they can overwhelm managers and staff. Operational protocols should be developed that flag urgent e-mail messages so that the recipient, usually the manager, can identify what is a priority and respond appropriately. E-mail senders tend to copy numerous other individuals. This wastes the time of people who have no need and perhaps little interest in viewing a barrage of messages extraneous to their tasks. The manager should emphasize that only those with a need to know should be copied on e-mail messages. In any event, everyone else is hitting the "delete" button.

When it comes to using the Internet and the Web, the manager should identify who needs to use tools such as the various browsers, search directories, and search engines and why they need to use these tools. The manager again needs a strategy. The manager should look at the tasks and assignments of individuals, groups, and teams to determine, with those involved, what Internet or Web capabilities can make a demonstrable difference in performance. One way to codify and document the need is through brief standard operating procedures (SOPs). These lay out the means by which various tasks are to be performed and can be placed on the intranet if widespread staff access is required. Also, use of the Internet and Web tools provides the opportunity for staff training and developing and creating or enhancing individual or group skills. All of these communication strategies share the common goal of improving productivity and performance.

Conclusion

When all is said and done, the basic tasks at which the manager must succeed are creating and sustaining a communications network to use and disseminate information. This involves identifying the basic communication needs of the archival unit as well as of the parent institution, understanding the specific information needs of staff and public, and creating a communications process that enables effective decision making and policy dissemination. No matter how simple it may be, an established communications process must be seen as accurate and consistent in its functioning.

Communication is all about trust. If the manager is perceived as fair, approachable, dependable, and competent by the unit, he or she will survive when those inevitable times of stress and turmoil arise.

Suggested Readings

There are too many books, articles, and theses on the theme of communication for any busy archival manager to identify, read, and absorb them all. The *Harvard Business Review* is an excellent one-stop source, particularly the compendium *Harvard Business Review on Effective Communication* (Cambridge, Mass.: Harvard Business School Press, 1999). The journal *Training and Development* regularly features articles on communication, particularly in a team-oriented environment.

The SAA annual meeting in August 2000 featured a session entitled "Collaboration and Communication: Practical Tools for Archival Managers" which focused on communications and teamwork.

Chapter 10

Managing Archival Facilities

The word *archives* comes from the Greek work *archeion*. In English as in Greek, it refers both to the official records created by an organization and to the building or facility where they are preserved and used. Archival repositories do more than provide space for the storage of records. They also carry out functions such as arrangement, reference, and conservation. In addition, archivists must choose equipment and supplies to furnish the archival facility. It is the responsibility of the archival administrator to secure a facility that meets minimal archival standards and that is furnished with the equipment and supplies needed to carry out fundamental archival activities. Because the storage environment can be the most cost-effective tool in preserving the holdings, preventing damage, and minimizing deterioration, it is critical that archival facilities meet environmental standards. Although this chapter is directed primarily to archives with a multiperson staff, the concepts can be applied to one-person repositories with limited space.

General Facility Requirements

Regardless of the type or repository, all facilities should attempt to meet certain standards:

1. Archival repositories should maintain a constant temperature and humidity wherever records are stored or used. No absolute temperature is optimum. In general, cooler temperatures and drier relative humidity are desirable for preservation of records. For example, storage at 50 degrees Fahrenheit will provide improved longevity over 68 degrees by as much as five times. Lowering the temperature improves preservation. However, priorities compete when it comes to selecting temperature and relative humidity for storage and use of holdings. What temperature is good for longevity? What is good for use and the user? What is economically feasible and practical? For paper-based holdings, managers and archivists should try not to exceed 68 degrees in a storage environment with a relative humidity (RH) between 35 and 45 percent.

   However, there are some reasons why this might not work for a specific repository, or why other conditions might be specified for certain holdings. For example, mixed collections last longest in storage at temperatures much lower than 68 degrees and at a relative humidity as low as 30 percent. However, when records stored at lower temperatures are used, the manager must be concerned about not passing the dew point to avoid condensation on the surface of unprotected items. Film and color photographic materials should be stored at lower temperatures. Experts recommend storage at 35 or 25 degrees Fahrenheit and 35 percent RH depending on the condition of the photographic materials.

   Environmental systems should be developed that can accommodate the records' needs in one area at lower temperatures and the comfort of people at higher temperatures in a processing and research area. If it is not possible to separate the conditions of storage and use areas, then find a temperature that will be comfortable, making the lowest practical storage temperature the lowest tolerable temperature for humans—somewhere in the high sixties. The air circulation and how much air is blowing on people will affect how they feel at a given temperature. Repositories that cannot achieve recommended standards should attempt to minimize temperature and humidity fluctuations by using air conditioners, humidifiers, and dehumidifiers depending upon seasonal requirements.

2. If the archives is part of a larger building, it should be located in an area offering optimal conditions. Damp basements and dry attics should be avoided. If possible, the repository should be located away from exposed water pipes or bathrooms because of the risk of flooding and water damage.
3. Work areas should be well lit, while light should be kept at lower levels in records' storage areas. There should be no windows in storage areas; if there are, they should all have curtains or blinds. All fluorescent lights and outside windows should have protective ultraviolet filters.
4. All repositories should be protected against unauthorized entry and theft. Outside entrances should be minimized, and entry doors securely locked. The archivist should maintain control of all keys. An alternative to the traditional lock is access by numbered keypads or magnetic cards. Although more expensive to install, these systems can be changed more easily and less expensively than those using keys. An intrusion alarm should be installed; it can be supplemented by security guards on twenty-four-hour duty.
5. The fire detection and suppression system will, in part, be dictated by local fire codes. A fire alarm system that can be triggered manually or automatically should operate twenty-four hours a day. Ionization or photoelectric smoke detectors that send an alarm automatically to a fire station or to a twenty-four-hour emergency service are preferred. When planning a fire detection and suppression system, it is important to obtain the services of a fire engineer familiar with archives and applicable National Fire Protection Association (NFPA) codes. Generally, a wet pipe aqueous suppression system is recommended rather than a gaseous fire suppression system, except under special circumstances such as in cold storage vaults or around materials at great risk from water damage. Experts can provide advice on whether gases such as FM200 or Inergen are appropriate for use. Also, pollutants and particulates should be kept to levels that minimize their impact on holdings.

6. Facility management should include an integrated pest-management program (IPM) along with an environmental monitoring program. For information, contact the Preservation Policy and Services Division, National Archives and Records Administration, which has developed an aggressive protocol for dealing with this issue.
7. Finally, repositories should be located in areas that are easily reached by the actual or potential clientele.

Components of an Archives Facility

All repositories should be organized and/or constructed to carry out archival activities: appraisal, acquisition, arrangement, description, reference, outreach, and conservation. These activities can be associated with the following functional areas: administration, technical services, public services, records storage, and common areas. Archival administrators must understand the archival activities and the building functions and ensure that the parent institution provides a facility to meet the repository's needs. (See figure 10-1.)

In addition to general needs, each functional area will have specific requirements:

ADMINISTRATION

- Entry foyer with space for a secretary-receptionist
- Offices with standard office equipment including desks, chairs, filing cabinets, telephones, photocopying machine, typewriters, fax modems, and computers
- Storage area for office supplies

TECHNICAL SERVICES

- Areas with standard office equipment and additional work space for arrangement and description
- Loading dock for deliveries
- Work tables and shelving for temporary storage of records and sorting equipment
- Computer terminal(s) for administrative and archival work
- Conservation equipment and space appropriate to the staff's

Figure 10-1 Building Functions

Administration
- Planning
- Financial management
- Personnel management
- Public relations

Public Services
- Reference services
- Exhibits
- Copying
- Public programs

Technical Services
- Acquisition
- Appraisal
- Arrangement
- Description
- Conservation

Records Storage
- Storage of all types of archival materials

Common Areas
- Bathrooms
- Hallways
- Lunchroom/lounge
- Space for utilities and equipment

abilities as well as the archives' budgetary constraints

- Isolation area for new archival holdings pending checks for insect or mold infestation
- Vaults for high-value items or those requiring cold storage

Public Services

- Welcoming, pleasant reading room with an adequate number of comfortable chairs and desks large enough to hold both records being used and the researcher's notes and designed so that researchers can be monitored by someone in the room or in adjacent offices
- Copies of common reference material and finding aids including a computer terminal for access to databases
- Equipment and separate areas for using audiovisual materials
- Space for the secure storage of coats and briefcases outside the reading room

- An exhibit area located near the main entrance to the facility (optional)
- Conference or meeting rooms

Common Areas

- An adequate number of bathrooms for staff and researchers
- Hallways large enough for the movement of both researchers and archival records

Records Storage

- Floors strong enough to support the shelving and records that will be placed in the facility. The necessary floor load will vary depending upon whether standard or compact, mobile shelving is used
- Storage areas with as few doors as possible to prevent unauthorized access
- Elevators suitable for transporting records in a multilevel stack
- Records storage located away from possible water hazards such as pipes or bathrooms, even if this is not possible for the entire archival facility

Space Planning and Design

Each of these areas has different but equally important functions. Archivists must understand the functions, their relationships, and how the different areas interact, so that they can make the most efficient use of space and provide staff members with a facility that meets individual and institutional needs. (See figure 10-2.) Staff involved with a particular function should be engaged in the design and layout of that area. For example, staff would be sensitive to the path and workflow of records for security and preservation reasons, the need to keep food areas distant from storage areas, and the requirement that elevators and doors should be large enough to handle the largest carts.

The processing area should be adjacent to the storage area so that collections can be removed for processing and then returned to storage. However, the work area must be separated by walls and/or windows from the reading room so that talking and office noise will not disturb researchers.

Figure 10-2 Functional Relationships Matrix

	Curator's Office	Director's Office	Special Projects Office (Unassigned)	Recreation Area	Meeting Room/Classroom	Kitchen	Lounge/Lunchroom	Quiet Reading Room	Reference/Consultation Area	Photoduplication & Supply Storage	Processing Workroom	Collection Storage	Preservation Laboratory	Loading Dock
Curator's Office														
Director's Office	2													
Special Projects Office (Unassigned)	2	3												
Reception Area (Exhibits)	2	2	2											
Meeting Room/ Classroom	3	2	3	2										
Kitchen	3	2	3	3	1									
Lounge/ Lunchroom	3	2	3	3	3	1								
Quiet Reading Room	2	2	3	2	2	3	2							
Reference/ Consultation Area	1	1	2	2	2	3	2	1						
Photoduplication & Supply Storage	2	3	2	1	3	3	3	2	2					
Processing Workroom	1	3	2	3	3	3	2	3	2	1				
Collection Storage	3	3	3	3	3	3	3	2	2	3	3			
Preservation Laboratory	3	3	3	3	3	3	3	3	3	3	3	2		
Loading Dock	3	3	3	3	3	3	3	3	3	3	3	2	1	

1 Immediate Adjacency Required

2 Proximity Required

3 Proximity Not Required

The reading room at the Austin History Center provides a comfortable research environment that has adequate lighting, space for researchers, and resources placed for ease of use. Austin History Center, Austin Public Library

The placement of staff offices depends largely upon function. Staff with processing responsibilities should be located close to the archives storage area but should not be directly accessible to researchers. The offices of reference personnel should be close to the storage area and the entrance, while providing direct supervision of and access to the reading room. Administrative offices should be located away from the reading room and storage areas, but close to the entrance.

The reading room should be designed with only one entrance/exit and so that people leaving the reading room pass by the office or desk of a staff member. The area should be carefully monitored whenever there is a researcher in the room. In larger facilities, a staff member or guard may be stationed in the room whenever it is open. Larger repositories may also have separate areas for microfilm readers or space to use computers, tape recorders, or photographic equipment.

Most repositories will have some common areas. Larger archives may have exhibit space, meeting rooms, or theaters. Such space should be carefully integrated into the overall facility, but should not, under normal circumstances, be directly accessible from the reading room.

A stack area at the Historical Society of Western Pennsylvania that needs more storage space. HISTORICAL SOCIETY OF WESTERN PENNSYLVANIA

Allocating Space

How much space is needed to operate an archival program? The amount of floor space, measured in square footage, needed for each of the five functions will depend upon a number of factors:

1. The size of the collection;
2. The number of staff members;
3. The number of tasks for which the archives is responsible; and
4. The number of researchers and other clients who are served.

Although standard measurements are used in planning new buildings, the manner in which a building is organized may have a major impact on whether space can be allocated in the most efficient manner.

In planning storage space, an archival administrator can expect to store approximately 1.5 cubic feet of records for each square foot allocated to storage, assuming the use of standard shelves with aisles between each range. The use of mobile, compact shelving can nearly

A stack area at the Historical Society of Western Pennsylvania after the installation of compact shelving. The shelving allows for better collection storage, collection growth, and easier access to materials.
HISTORICAL SOCIETY OF WESTERN PENNSYLVANIA

triple the storage capacity to nearly 4.5 cubic feet of records for each square foot of storage.

Standard office space should be allotted at approximately 100 to 125 square feet for each staff member. If the person has technical services responsibility, this amount should be increased by 50 to 75 percent to accommodate storage of materials being processed. This space can be arranged as individual offices or as a large open space with partitions utilizing modular furniture. Open space with movable partitions offers greater flexibility, while individual offices give staff members greater privacy. The amount of office space allocated to particular individuals may be adjusted upward depending upon their responsibilities and space needs. For example, reference archivists may require additional space if they spend time in the office interviewing researchers or holding conferences with reference staff.

Space in the reference area should average approximately 40 to 50 square feet for each researcher. This will include space for one desk, one chair, and a free area around the desk. In addition to this space, a certain amount of floor space must be made available for card catalogs, indexes, reference books, and other finding aids, as well as for permitted personal equipment, such as personal computers and scanners, and for book trucks and records in use. Additional space will be needed for researchers using oversized holdings or in a repository with significant quantities of oversized materials coming to the research room.

Archival Equipment

In addition to space, all repositories require a minimum of equipment to operate effectively. An archives may begin with cast-off filing cabinets, but these should not substitute for standard metal shelving. (See figure 10-3.) For standard paper records, 18- to 22- gauge metal shelving with a powder-coated finish is recommended. The archival administrator should choose shelves designed to hold approximately 150 to 200 pounds. A common arrangement for repositories using records center boxes are shelves that are 15 inches deep and 42 inches long, arranged in bays six shelves high with aisles at least 32 inches wide. In this configuration, the metal uprights holding the shelves in place should be able to withstand a weight of 900 pounds, the average weight that can normally be stored on six shelves.

The use of records center boxes maximizes the existing floor space. Although compact shelving can be used to greatly increase available space, consider these space-saving alternatives for standard shelving as well. One method is the use of double-depth shelving with one box stored behind another. This technique eliminates one aisle but requires employees to move one box to gain access to the one behind it. It should only be erected in situations where material is not heavily used. Another alternative is high-rise shelving. Installing ranges more than six shelves high will increase shelving density by taking advantage of unused vertical space. Access to tall shelving requires a suspended catwalk or a manual or machine-supported ladder or platform.

In addition to high-density shelving, most repositories need a variety of equipment for the storage of other types of boxes and materials. Repositories with large book collections will require library

Figure 10-3 Shelving Terminology

Aisle – The amount of open space between two ranges of shelving. Aisles can vary from 24 to 36 inches in width, but must be wide enough to maneuver trucks and to load and unload boxes and volumes.

Bay – A vertical row of shelves.

Compact Shelving (also called movable or mobile shelving) – A series of shelving ranges set on platforms. The platforms sit on tracks allowing the range to be moved manually or automatically right or left. Compact shelving allows a repository to use as little as one aisle for an entire records storage area, increasing the amount of material that can be stored in a given area.

Floor Loading – The number of pounds that a floor will support, usually given in pounds per square foot. The floor load will vary depending upon the type of building construction. The greater the shelving density, the higher the required floor load. Information on floor load is generally available from building specifications. If there is any doubt, a structural engineer should be consulted.

Gauge – Term used to describe the thickness of metal shelving. The lower the number, the thicker and stronger the metal.

Library Shelving (also called cantilever shelving) – Shelving supported only by uprights at the rear corners of the shelf. The shelf is attached to the uprights by hooks on the shelf. The holes on the upright are one inch apart, allowing for easy height adjustment of individual shelves. Library shelving is most often used for bound volumes and manuscript boxes. It is usually 36 inches in length and comes in a variety of depths.

Range – One row of shelving bays.

(continued)

Figure 10-3 continued

Records Center Shelving (also called industrial shelving) – Shelving supported by uprights at all four corners. The shelving is usually attached to the uprights by bolts and cannot be easily adjusted for varying heights. Standard records center shelving is 42 inches long and 15 inches deep, and it is designed to store three records center boxes per shelf. Some records center shelving is designed to hold six boxes, with one box stored behind another.

Shelving Density – The number of shelves that can be installed in a fixed amount of space. The number or width of the aisles or the height of the shelving can affect this amount.

shelving 36 inches long and 9 inches deep. (See figure 10-4.) The repository should purchase deeper shelving for oversized volumes so that they can lie flat, thus preserving their bindings. Some filing cabinets will probably be needed for storage of actively used subject files and for photograph storage. Also, flat, oversized file drawers are needed for oversized materials such as cartographic items, posters, and broadsides.

Repositories require a variety of office equipment: desks, office chairs, reading-room tables and seats, filing cabinets, bookshelves, and similar items. Such equipment is available from standard office suppliers, but items should be carefully evaluated to ensure that they meet specialized archival needs. For example, reading-room tables should provide a large tabletop for work space, and for security reasons they should be entirely open underneath with no panels or other barriers that might block a reading-room supervisor's view.

When purchasing new equipment, the archivist must choose from a variety of equipment and manufacturers. He or she should begin by collecting literature and information on a variety of equipment and companies. This should be followed by discussions with sales personnel who will be able to explain the different features of their products as well as pricing. The archivist should ask for the names of institutions that have used the equipment sold by particular companies. This

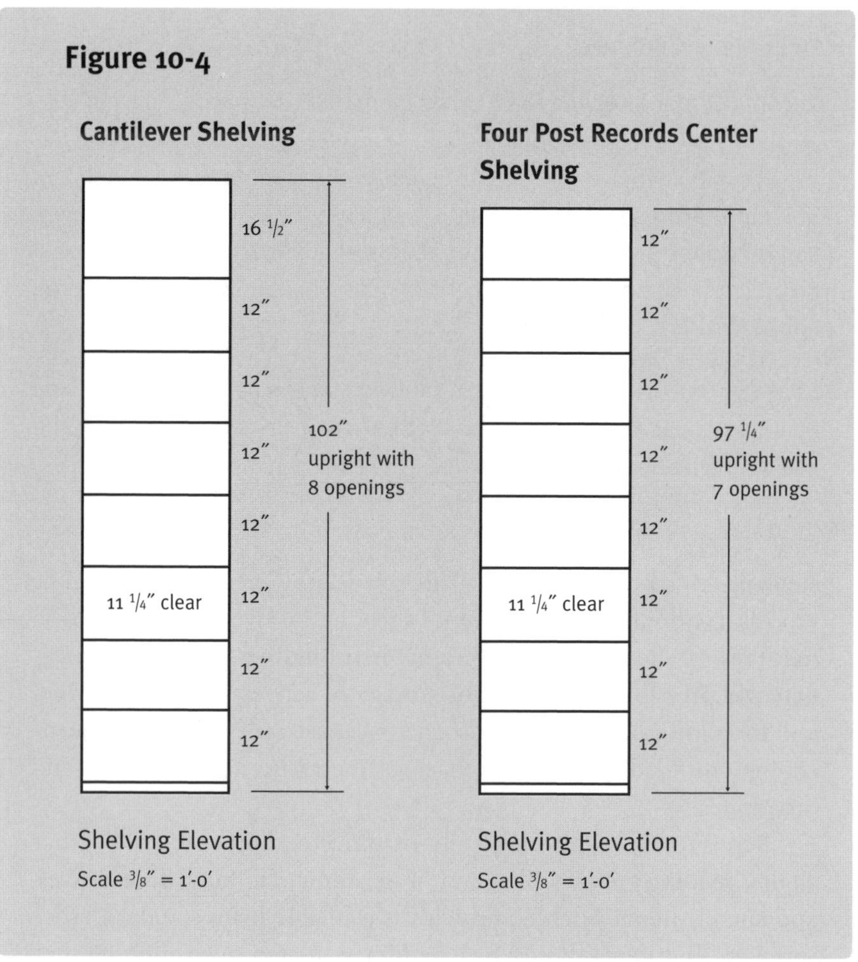

should be followed up by telephone calls and on-site visits to learn about customer satisfaction and the equipment's operational effectiveness. When more than one company manufactures equipment meeting institutional needs, and its vendors have comparable reputations, bids should be requested so that the archival manager can choose the lowest price.

If the repository's parent agency purchases its equipment from one particular manufacturer, and the manufacturer also makes products suitable for an archival environment, the archivist may wish to go no further in seeking new equipment. If this is not the case, the archivist may wish to find several companies that manufacture a wide range of equipment and seek bids on an entire package.

Archival Supplies

Archivists only periodically face the task of purchasing equipment, but they must continually buy supplies for many ongoing tasks. Supplies range from mundane items, such as stationery, pencils, and pens, to more specialized items including archival boxes, folders, and conservation supplies. In choosing supplies, the archival administrator must balance cost against the minimum standards needed to protect archival material. For standard office supplies that do not involve archival material, the only considerations are usefulness and price. However, items used in direct connection with archival material must not harm documents and should be able to slow their deterioration.

The usefulness of different archival products should be tested by direct comparison. Manufacturers of archival supplies generally provide samples, which can be compared for usefulness, quality, and archival stability. Technical information and specifications, if not included with archival supplies, must be requested and compared with similar products available in the marketplace, so that standards for archival supplies, such as the Photographic Activity Test (PAT) (ANSI) for containers for photographic materials, are consistently followed in all purchases. Archivists can contact a reputable conservation laboratory or the Society of American Archivists for assistance.

A range of products to choose from almost always confronts the archivist. By carefully evaluating those choices, he or she can purchase supplies that meet the archives' needs and are cost effective. Once the initial choice is made, the archivist should not assume that the repository can go on purchasing the same materials year after year with no further thought or concern. The archivist must continually evaluate supplies to ensure that they meet consistent standards. Unsatisfactory supplies should be returned to the manufacturer for replacement or credit. If not satisfied, the archivist should seek an alternate supplier.

In addition, the archivist should be alert for new or modified products that meet the repository's needs. New products may be found in announcements in professional literature or in catalogs or sales literature. Only by constant vigilance can the archival administrator hope to identify and purchase the highest quality and most cost-effective products.

Reviewing Space Needs

As repositories grow, archivists make decisions about the space they occupy while evaluating the larger issues affecting the archival facility. Sometimes a new staff member's work station is added here, a computer there, and a photocopying machine somewhere else. Growth by serendipity can have unexpected effects on both employee effectiveness and the working environment, if great care is not exercised. Space can become crowded; a photocopying machine can raise the ambient temperature of the room; or computer work stations can be poorly arranged.

Such problems should not be underestimated, and an archival administrator should constantly evaluate the facility to discover ways in which it can be used more effectively. In the same way that archivists plan an annual budget, they should frequently schedule a facility review. Is there sufficient space for the expected acquisition of archival collections during the next one, three, or five years? Do future budgets include funds for additional staff? Will there be sufficient space for these individuals? Are there plans to introduce a new office automation or computer system? If there is space for equipment, what is its most logical placement, and what impact will it have on departmental relationships?

Answers to questions like these can often be found through research in books and publications on facilities and equipment. While archival literature on such subjects is limited, a review of library and records management articles may prove extremely helpful. A thorough discussion with other staff members can also prove valuable, since their use of space and equipment provides them with insight into the relationships between the two.

If personal research and staff insight are insufficient, outside experts can help, starting with other archivists who have recently reorganized or renovated buildings. Their experience and insight can be combined with visits to their facilities for tours and discussion. Most repositories are part of larger organizations that may have facility personnel responsible for developing new buildings or supervising renovations. Their experience can be extremely valuable as they should be familiar with a variety of equipment and techniques to maximize space and plan for the relationships between different parts of the archives.

Other resources are available. For a fee, firms that specialize in space planning can review the space available, record the functions that occur within the space, and develop a logical and effective plan. Unfortunately, few of these companies have dealt specifically with archival repositories. Certainly their personnel will be able to apply their expertise from other projects, but archivists should take special care to ensure that the recommendations meet the repository's needs.

If funds are not available, and the repository has a specific problem that involves both space and equipment, an archives can sometimes call on one or more equipment manufacturers for advice. From work and experience in other libraries and archives, such firms can provide planning expertise. For example, shelving companies can make suggestions about the types and arrangements of shelving. They might suggest the installation of compact shelving to replace already existing shelves. Such advice can be extremely helpful, but the archival administrator must always remember that, along with giving advice, these companies are also seeking to sell their products.

Expanding the Facility

Archivists can carefully plan and reorganize existing space, but there will be times when the repository's need for work and/or storage space outstrips existing resources. When faced with such a dilemma, the archival manager must carefully develop a strategy that meets the archives' space needs. One alternative is to expand into adjacent space. Can other offices be moved to allow further expansion? Is such space suitable for archival purposes? Is expansion a politically viable solution within the structure of the parent institution? If the answer is yes to all of these questions, the archivist has found a solution to the space problems and can get on with planning for renovation and expansion.

If the answer to any of these questions is no, the archivist must seek other solutions. If storage space is the major concern, the repository can seek to compress its records storage through the use of microfilm, microfiche, or digital imaging. These, however, are expensive alternatives and are available in only few select cases. Another alternative is to develop off-site storage for records. This may solve short-term space needs, but it creates other problems of access or perhaps inadequate environmental controls. With large increases in staff or holdings, the archivist must seek a different facility to meet both immediate and long-term needs.

Whether the repository is expanding into additional space or planning for a new facility, much of the planning and preparation will be the same. The manager's first step must be to evaluate the short-term and long-term space needs of the archives in conjunction with its long-range plan. What is the current number of staff members? What changes in staffing are expected in the next one, five, or ten years? A second area of concern is the expected increase in the size of the archival collection. This cannot be predicted with absolute accuracy, but statistics on annual increases in the collection can provide the parameters for future space needs. If the repository has not collected such data, annual growth can be extrapolated by dividing the total volume of the collection by the number of years that the institution has been in existence. (See figure 10-5.)

A third concern in future planning is providing space for current and projected researchers. Such planning is facilitated by keeping accurate records of the number of researchers who visit the archives and projecting the amount of growth over a period of years. Future needs can be projected in a fashion similar to that used for storage space. When planning space requirements for researchers, the archives administrator should take into account not only the reading room but also the space required for additional bathrooms, handicapped access, areas to store coats and bags, and other needs connected with this function. Overlooking such areas leads to overcrowding of facilities, both for staff and researchers.

A fourth concern should be the security of the collection. Current security measures should be reviewed. Even if they have been adequate, planning for a new facility will allow the administrative archivist to

Figure 10-5 Projecting Future Storage Needs

1. Current Volume of Records Stored: 3,100 Cubic Feet

2. Annual Increase: $\frac{3{,}100\text{cf}}{10\text{ years}}$ = 310 cf of annual increase

3. If the repository must plan its new facility so that it has space for an additional fifteen years it will need:

    310 cf per year
    x 15 years
    4,650 additional cubic feet of storage

4. Total Storage Needs:

    3,100 cubic feet of current records storage
    + 4,650 cubic feet of additional storage
    7,750 cubic feet is the total needed for the next fifteen years

upgrade security measures and install more modern equipment. Because of the specialized nature of security systems, it may be helpful to seek the advice of a security consultant.

Finally, space plans should include current or new archival functions developed through institutional planning. These might include exhibit areas, conference rooms, lecture halls, conservation laboratories, and audiovisual use areas. Again, current and future space needs should be projected. However, such projections will be speculative in nature and hard to defend on the basis of past statistics. This task will be made easier by linking the long-range plan of the repository with building plans.

Once all the data on current and future needs have been collected, the archival administrator can indicate to the repository's parent

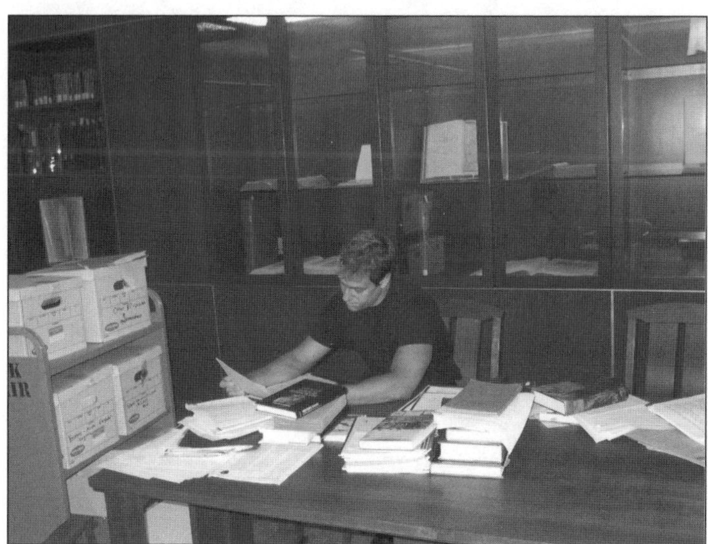

Researchers need ample space so that they can organize their work and create a safe working environment for materials. UNIVERSITY OF NEVADA LAS VEGAS

organization the amount of additional space that must be added to its current facility or the total amount needed in a new or different building. Negotiating for new space is a political process requiring both skill and nerve. In making a presentation, the archivist must strongly support needs for space. If factual and statistical evidence supports these needs, such a stance is made easier. Archivists should never fear asking for the resources needed to do their work, and space is one of those commodities that an archives needs to function.

If the building concept is approved, the archival manager must discuss alternative means of financing the facility. Will funds be allocated by the parent institution, or will money be raised from donors or private foundations? Such decisions are usually out of the archivist's hands, but in some cases may become the archivist's responsibility.

Preservation Concerns

In planning for an expanded facility, a number of preservation concerns should be taken into account. For example, every effort should be made to separate processing and other functions from records storage to provide the environment that benefits the records and is minimally influenced by the needs of people. Wherever records are stored, used, processed, or exhibited, food and drink should be not be allowed

A new facility should be sited a minimum of five feet above and a hundred feet from any hundred-year flood plain area, or it should be protected by an appropriate flood wall that conforms to local or regional building codes. Records should be stored at least three inches above the floor surface. No fountains, pools, or standing water should be allowed over or adjacent to areas where records are stored, processed, used, or exhibited. If there are concerns about potential water damage in records storage areas, installation of a water detection system should be considered. The facility must be kept under positive air pressure, especially in the areas adjacent to the loading dock. Loading docks should have an air supply and exhaust system that is separate from the remainder of the facility.

Areas where records are used, processed, stored, or exhibited must be isolated from sources of pollutants and particulates. Doors to the records areas must not open directly onto the loading dock, machine rooms, locations where woodworking or painting take place, or other similar areas. The air intakes and returns must be designed so that lower quality air and environment cannot affect the records areas, and they must vent directly to the outdoors.

The following materials should not be permitted in the areas where records are used, processed, exhibited, and stored, including vaults:

a. Cellulose nitrate lacquers and adhesives;
b. Polyurethane products, including paints, varnishes, and foams;
c. Acid-curing silicone sealants and adhesives;
d. Sulfur-containing materials that could release SO2;
e. Pressure-sensitive adhesives that release VOCs;
f. Unstable chlorine polymers (PVCs);
g. Formaldehyde-emitting compounds, such as might be found in particle boards;
h. Vinyls; and
i. Oil-based paints and varnishes.

Certain industry and international standards are useful in developing preservation strategies. These include NISO TROL-1995, which provides environmental guidelines for the storage of paper records, and ANSI/NISO Z39.79.2001, establishing environmental conditions for exhibiting library and archival materials.

Working with Architects, Engineers, and Contractors

Once the parent institution approves the release of space needed for expansion or construction of a new facility, the archival administrator becomes involved in an odyssey of education and frustration. Almost immediately, the archivist will be thrust into a world of construction terms, blueprints, and building personnel who have little or no knowledge of what an archives is or does. The archivist's ability to learn quickly, to communicate effectively, and to educate architects and builders working on the building may mean the difference between a carefully constructed, fully functional facility and one that requires significant changes or operational compromise once it is completed. It is critical that the archival manager be a member of the building design team. The team should also involve staff members representing the key functions, as well as facilities and preservation. A preservation staff member should provide technical expertise on the needs of the holdings, assistance on achieving the correct environment, and information on selecting the furnishings to minimize off-gassing. If a preservation specialist or conservator is not on staff, the archival manager should ensure that a preservation consultant is hired for the building period.

One of the first tasks that the archivist confronts is the selection of an architect/engineer(s). The archivist should seek an architect and engineer experienced in the specialized needs of an archives or research library, and every effort should be made to visit buildings designed by the architect and the engineer and to talk with people occupying those facilities. Using an architect or engineer who already has working knowledge of archival and library functions will, in the long run, save the archivist time and energy and should result in a more functional building. The archivist should also be involved in negotiating the contracts for the architect and engineer needed for the project so that everyone understands exactly what has been agreed. While project proposals obviously must take into account cost, quality considerations must be paramount. The primary contract will call for designing the building or space within a larger facility, but the architect and engineer can also be asked to

- Do a program study to evaluate the amount of space needed for different building functions.
- Do a site comparison and analysis between two or more possible locations for a new archival facility.
- Select additional equipment such as furniture or shelving.

Such items should be discussed and responsibilities assigned before agreeing to a contract.

If the architect or the engineers have not worked on an archival facility, the archivist must begin an education program explaining various archival functions, how they relate to one another, and the amount of space needed to carry them out. At an early stage, the archivist should create a list of functional areas that must be included in the new building and the amount of space needed for each. The list should be accompanied by a program statement outlining archival activities and their relationships, which can be used to educate both architects and contractors. At the same time, the architect should outline relevant building and fire codes that affect both renovations and new construction and how these may affect the archival facility.

If the preliminary planning has been thorough, this process should go smoothly and quickly. In designing the building, the architect and engineer will combine this information with other factors such as cost, volume of space, and design to come up with a final plan. During the design phase, the architect will present three successive sets of drawings and blueprints. At each stage the archivist must carefully review these documents and suggest changes or corrections. The archivist should not be afraid to ask the architect or engineer questions. Archivists who are unfamiliar with blueprints or who have little experience with planning buildings should call upon their institution's property department, members of the repository staff, friends, or colleagues to go over the plans for comments and suggestions. They may also want to consider hiring a consultant with experience in reviewing library or archival facilities. Archivists can educate themselves through reading and research. *The Dictionary of Architecture and Construction* by Cyril Harris may be helpful. (See suggested readings at the end of this chapter.)

Changes in the plans are fairly easy to make during the early planning stages. However, as time passes, it becomes increasingly difficult, if not impossible, so it is incumbent upon the archivist to carefully review the plans before they become finalized and construction begins. Great care must be taken in evaluating the location of functional archival areas, the placement and size of doors and windows, the width of aisles, and similar details. Although it is impossible to foresee how a facility will operate while it is only in the blueprint stage, the archivist must make a careful and considered attempt to ensure that it meets the institution's needs.

Building Construction

The building plans go through several stages until the final plan is accepted. After the plan is complete, the institution may call upon the contractor it normally uses to give a cost estimate or ask for bids from a number of firms. The bidding process will reflect the architectural and engineering plans, including specifications for such things as heating, air conditioning and climate control, fire protection, and security systems.

If the repository has dealt with subcontractors for specific services such as climate control or fire protection, the archivist can request that such vendors be used by the contractor who is making the bid. He or she can seek recommendations and suggestions from other archivists or from conservation laboratories or consultants when the archives has had no previous contact with such specialists. Such efforts must be completed before the bidding takes place so that the subcontractor's costs can be included. If there is more than one bid, the institution must compare the bids based upon cost as well as upon the reputation of the contracting firms under consideration.

The archivist's work is not done once construction begins. He or she should visit the site on a regular basis to check progress and compare the blueprints with the actual construction. The archivist should keep in close contact with the contractor since there will still be some decisions to make, particularly if construction falls behind schedule or the contractor discovers major difficulties in meeting the specifications given in the plans.

The result of all of these efforts should be a new or remodeled building that is efficiently designed and will meet the needs of the repository for many years to come. Such is the result of careful planning by the archivist, the involvement of a creative architect, and the work of skilled craftspeople.

Conclusion

While not every archivist will build or remodel an archival facility, all archivists are faced with planning for the best use of their facilities as well as for the purchase of supplies and equipment. Such decisions have a significant impact on the total program and should always be carefully considered. Through applied common sense backed by thorough research and information gleaned from conservation experts, the archivist should be able to make decisions that lead to positive results and an improved archival facility.

Suggested Readings

Archivists planning new facilities should consult Michele F. Pacifico, "The National Archives at College Park," *Government Information Quarterly* 13, no. 2 (1996); Howard P. Lowell, "Building a Public Archives in Delaware for the Twenty-First Century," *American Archivist* 60, no. 2 (Spring 1997); and Jeannette Woodward, *Countdown to a New Library: Managing the Building Project* (Chicago and London: American Library Association, 2000). An interesting article on renovating facilities is Shirley C. Spragge, "Old Wine in Old Bottles: Renovating an Old Building for an Archives," in *The Archival Imagination: Essays in*

Honor of Hugh A. Taylor (Ottawa, Canada: Association of Canadian Archivists, 1992).

From the archival perspective, Mary Lynn Ritzenthaler, *Preserving Archives and Manuscripts* (Chicago: Society of American Archivists, 1993), defines the core elements in an archival preservation program with information on procedures, supplies, and equipment included.

Chapter 11

Financial Management

Whatever the size of an archives, it consumes resources, both material and human.[1] It needs to account for the resources it uses and to plan for the acquisition of the resources needed to continue its operations into the future. Beyond accounting and planning for operations at the current level, financial management is critical to any effort to expand, grow, or perhaps even escape from the archival "cycle of poverty."

Organizations normally account for their income and expenses to three major audiences: an external regulatory or legal authority, higher management within the organization's parent institution, and the managers of the organization itself. Each has its own uses for financial management data, and these dictate the form accountability must take.

External authorities can include the Internal Revenue Service and other governmental bodies, as well as foundations and endowments that normally require financial statements in return for grants or other funds. Whether the management of an archives reports to higher authority within a parent institution or to a board of trustees, such authorities require evidence that the staff of the archives is carrying out its responsibilities in accordance with approved policies. Finally, managers within the archives need accurate financial information to document performance, to make the best use of limited resources, and to reveal trends in operations that may require their attention.

---

1 This chapter focuses principally on the financial obligations of relatively small repositories, i.e. those that do not have a professional budget and accounting staff, and whose operations do not require capital budgets and other instruments used by large institutions.

Understanding the Financial Environment

As in every other aspect of management, finance requires a careful review and understanding of an organization's operating environment. How does the archives acquire the money with which it operates? What are the sources of that money, and what procedures are involved in obtaining it? On the other side of the ledger are expenses. How does the organization expend the resources allocated to it? What authorities must grant permission before the organization commits resources to equipment, personnel, facilities, or other costs? What requirements does the allocating authority impose for accounting for the use of those revenues?

The answers to these questions represent the financial control function of management; finance is equally important in the planning function. Will the demands on an archives' staff or facility grow over the next three years? Five years? If so, will the archives be in a position to deal with these increases by adding personnel, enlarging facilities, or otherwise expanding? Or will it be forced to retrench, to turn away collections because of lack of space, or to handle its materials poorly because of inadequate staff? Financial planning is essential in mapping out the real costs of change over time and for alerting management (within the archives), resource allocators, and possibly other constituent groups (researchers) of the archives' efforts to cope with change. Financial management, like other management functions, operates within a perpetual cycle, with plans and operations being adapted as required by changing circumstances.

Financial Planning

Managers must fully integrate financial planning with plans for the acquisition and use of personnel, facilities, and other resources.[2] (See chapter 5 for a more thorough discussion of planning processes.) Once an organization has established its objectives for the period

2 Archives that exist within larger institutions will have to pay particular attention to coordi-

covered by the long-range or strategic plan, it must answer an important financial question: How much money will it take to implement that plan? Identifying this figure, even in approximate terms, is essential for the planner. An unrealistic project is best stopped before money, time, and effort are wasted and before it becomes a sacred cow with a vested right to survive. On the other hand, virtually nothing is lost by calculating the costs of projects for which funding is uncertain; in the event of an unexpected windfall, the organization should at least have a general idea of its objectives. A "wish list" can be useful in convincing resource allocators that the archives' management is actively thinking about the future; creating such a list costs very little.

The plan—and its attendant costs—must then be matched against the revenues *likely to be available* to the organization. At this point the manager may find it desirable to make two or three projections about revenue: an optimistic one, a pessimistic one, and an intermediate one. Note the absence of the designation "realistic." All revenue projections, even the extremes, should be realistic in that they reflect possibilities that might actually occur. For example, an organization applying for grant money to accomplish a project is realistic in calculating the availability of the requested funds in its optimistic forecast, especially if it has successfully competed for grants in the past. Simply hoping that some unknown benefactor will appear is not realistic.

Fiscal resources must be prioritized. The organization must know which operations have the first claim on money coming in, which come next, and so on. In most instances, current operations—being able to sustain ongoing efforts—come first. Expansion and new projects must compete for whatever is left. The emphasis, though it may seem to discourage innovation and experimentation, is entirely appropriate for archives, which are essentially conserving institutions. Their managers would be irresponsible in adopting financial plans that expose their operations or their holdings to risk.

---

nating their planning — including financial planning — in accordance with the procedures and policies of the parent institution.

Budgeting

Budgets are useful both for planning and controlling funds, as products of the planning process, and as tools by which managers control the expenditure of resources. Effective budgeting is part of a multiyear process in which financial planning is done several (perhaps as many as three to five) years in advance of activity, and budgets are prepared and approved in the year before activity takes place. Though changes in a plan or project may require deviations from the budget, the manager's goal should be to limit these as much as possible.

Archives should establish a fiscal year, if one is not mandated by a parent organization. Fiscal years may start at any time and may be changed (the federal fiscal cycle starts on October 1 and ends on September 30). If the practical reasons for establishing a fiscal year are not readily apparent, the IRS has provided a regulatory one: organizations claiming tax-exempt status must report their income and expenses according to an exact fiscal year.

Let us assume a fiscal year based on the calendar year, January 1 to December 31. An organization's multiyear cycle of planning, budgeting, and operating for the fiscal years 2002 through 2004 might have three budgets in preparation at any one time, each going through different stages of development. (See figure 11-1.)

Thus, during fiscal year 2002, while money planned and budgeted for in earlier years is being spent, the budget for fiscal year 2003 should be in preparation, as should plans for fiscal year 2004. The differences in the stages for the latter years reflect the fact that plans for 2002 must be narrowed more precisely as the moment comes for money to be approved and released. While the exact sequence of steps will vary from institution to institution, as will the procedures involved in preparing, presenting, and defending proposals that must be approved by higher authorities, the cyclical, continuous interaction of planning and budgeting should be universally applicable.

Though in larger organizations several budgets, especially capital and operating budgets, may be in use at any one time, most archival organizations will use only the latter. Simply stated, an operating budget is a projection, for a defined period of time, of the expenses needed to operate a program or operation and the revenues required

Figure 11-1 Multiyear Cycle of Planning, Budgeting, and Operating

YEAR	JAN 1	JULY 1	DEC 31
2002 (current year)	Funds released	Midyear review	End-of-year accounting
2003 (budget preparation year)	Budget prepared	Review	Approval
2004 (planning year)	Planning preparation	Feasibility studies and cost estimates	Review and defense

to meet those expenses. The budget identifies in general terms sources of both. A sample budget is found in figure 11-2.

What can be learned about Sample County's Historical Society from its budget? For one thing, it apparently occupies donated or otherwise free property, leaving it only to pay its telephone bill. Its greatest expenditure is for the service of its two part-time employees. In 2002 and 2003, the society budgeted for relatively heavy equipment expenses (for personal computers, perhaps?). It seems to finance travel, possibly to a professional meeting, on a biennial basis.

Much of this is merely accounting information; what about planning? For the most part, this seems to be a conservative organization that produces its budget by taking last year's figures and adding a guess for inflation to produce next year's estimates. There are indications, however, of a more active approach. The figures suggest that the equipment purchases were planned and sequential. Moreover, it appears that the society has grown impatient with merely hoping for small annual

Figure 11-2 Line-Item Budget of the Sample County Historical Society Fiscal Year 2003 (January 1 through December 31)

PREPARED: AUGUST 2002

Income	Budgeted 2001	Actual 2001	Budgeted 2002	Estimated 2002	Budgeted 2003
Dues	$17,500	$17,000	$18,500	$18,000	$18,500
Gift Shop	600	100	500	200	500
Donations	1,300	1,400	1,500	1,600	4,500
TOTAL	19,400	18,500	19,800	19,800	23,000

Expenses	Budgeted 2001	Actual 2001	Budgeted 2002	Estimated 2002	Budgeted 2003
Salaries:					
Director (p/t)	8,500	8,500	8,700	8,700	9,000
Assistant (p/t)	3,700	3,700	3,900	3,900	4,100
Employee Benefits	2,000	2,200	2,400	2,400	2,500
Trustees' Expenses	400	430	500	675	550
Supplies:					
Office	500	535	600	400	750
Preservation	600	615	650	600	700
Equipment	150	150	1,500	1,650	1,100
Printing	350	400	450	500	600
Postage	300	325	400	475	525
Telephone	300	360	350	400	425
Subscriptions	200	180	150	150	200
Memberships	180	200	250	175	300
Professional:					
Auditor	350	350	350	350	400
Legal	200	200	0	0	0
Travel/Conference	1,200	1,140	300	150	1,200
TOTAL	18,930	18,655	19,750	19,675	21,500

increases in revenue through membership dues. The society is planning for a major increase in income from gifts and bequests — and should have a plan to achieve that goal. Without such a plan, this budget entry is likely to be nothing more than wishful thinking. Other points of interest include the absence of legal expenses (real and budgeted) after 2001. Has the society found a local attorney to volunteer legal services as needed? Or was the 2001 legal expense unusual and therefore not worthy of being figured into budgets for succeeding years?

Types of Budgets

The Sample County Historical Society budget reviewed above is an example of perhaps the most traditional of budget formats, the line-item budget. In this form, broad categories of expenditures are itemized, without linking those expenditures to the purpose or programs for which they were spent and without explicit links to stated organizational objectives.

The line-item budget is a useful tool and likely will remain in use for a long time. It provides information on trends in expenditures (Which is rising faster, salaries or the cost of maintaining a facility?), and it is relatively simple to prepare. Nevertheless, its failure to link expenses and objectives, or expenses and accomplishments, limits its value, especially for organizations that expect or desire a significant change in their operations or their operating environment. If, for example, an organization's costs for equipment have increased only minimally over the years, successive line-item budgets would show this pattern. The decision to automate the organization's functions would almost certainly be reflected by a noticeable, if not dramatic, increase in equipment costs. The line-item format does not permit this increase to be explained or justified by information on the expected improvements to be achieved by this atypical increase in costs. By highlighting increased costs without providing a rationale for them, line-item budgeting can endanger a project rather than enhance its chances of gaining approval.

One solution to this problem was the development of program budgeting, in which salaries, materials, equipment, and, where applicable, building construction or maintenance, are not consolidated for the entire organization but charged to various programs. In an archival setting, major programs might include general administration, acquisition and appraisal, collection maintenance, preservation, user services, and outreach. Though some organizations may choose to use either line-item or program budgeting exclusively, they can serve as complementary tools, each providing its own view of the organization's activities. What would a program budget for the Sample County Historical Society look like? (See figure 11-3.)

The figures allocated to these various programs and functions should match the totals recorded in the line-item budget. For the small institution where the staff is employed in a number of duties, this may require seemingly arbitrary efforts to account for time spent on each duty and additional effort to allocate costs. In this example, all telephone and membership expenses are accounted for centrally, while supplies, subscriptions, and equipment have been charged to specific functions. Is the more precise allocation worth the effort? Yes, if the information obtained provides a better—or even different—look at the organization's activities, or if it makes it easier for the organization to attract additional resources. Note, for example, that 25 percent of the limited money available to the historical society is charged to general administration. Is this too high? A definitive answer is hard to provide, but suppose one of the organization's goals is to provide more and better service to researchers. One way to achieve this would be to acquire more money for additional staff. An alternative would be to have the more highly paid director turn over more administrative duties to the less highly paid assistant, freeing up more of the director's time for user service or other professional duties. In addition to meeting management's objectives, this might be a better use of the society's talent. Thus, program budgeting can reflect how operations reflect, or contradict, stated objectives.

An easy way for management to respond to pressure to cut administrative costs would be to allocate costs for telephone and other services to the functional programs of the society. How much does this reduce telephone costs? Not at all, of course. Such apparent legerdemain is not always deceptive or illegitimate. Suppose, for example, that most of the long-distance calls made by the society are

Figure 11-3 Program Budget of the Sample County Historical Society Fiscal Year 2003 (January 1 through December 31)

Program		Budgeted 2002		Budgeted 2003
General Administration				
Salaries and Benefits		$3,100		$3,200
Supplies		300		375
Equipment		300		220
Printing		100		150
Postage		200		250
Telephone		350		425
Subscriptions		0		0
Memberships		250		300
Professional		350		400
	(25%)	4,950	(24.8%)	5,350
Acquisition and Appraisal				
Salaries and Benefits		3,100		3,230
Supplies		100		125
Equipment		300		220
Printing		50		50
Postage		0		0
Telephone		0		0
Subscriptions		50		75
Memberships		0		0
Professional		0		0
	(18.2%)	3,600	(21.8%)	4,700
Collection Maintenance				
Salaries and Benefits		3,875		4,037.50
Supplies		100		125
Equipment		375		275
Printing		50		50
Postage		0		0
Telephone		0		0
Subscriptions		50		75
Memberships		0		0
Professional		0		0
	(22.5%)	4,450	(21.2%)	4,562.50

(continued)

Figure 11-3 continued

Program		Budgeted 2002		Budgeted 2003
Preservation				
Salaries and Benefits		2,325		2,422.50
Supplies		650		700
Equipment		225		165
Printing		50		50
Postage		0		0
Telephone		0		0
Subscriptions		50		50
Memberships		0		0
Professional		0		0
	(16.9%)	3,300	(15.8%)	3,397.50
User Services				
Salaries and Benefits		2,325		2,422.50
Supplies		75		100
Equipment		200		170
Printing		50		50
Postage		0		0
Telephone		0		0
Subscriptions		0		0
Memberships		0		0
Professional		0		0
	(13.6%)	2,650	(12.8%)	2,742.50
Outreach				
Salaries and Benefits		2775		807.50
Supplies		25		25
Equipment		100		50
Printing		150		250
Postage		200		275
Telephone		0		0
Subscriptions		0		0
Memberships		0		0
Professional		0		0
	(6.4%)	1,250	(6.5%)	1,407.50

in pursuit of collections. Why not allocate part of the telephone bill to acquisition and appraisal? Such valid examples aside, there is no point in denying the obvious: budgets can be manipulated to show what management wants them to show. Reallocation of costs to reflect more accurately the use of revenues is one thing; reallocating costs to give an impression of nonexistent savings is another. To say that the latter happens all the time, or "everybody does it," does not resolve the issues raised by manipulative budget management.

Setting Priorities

Program budgeting can reflect an organization's priorities. The first priority, of course, must be for the society to continue to exist and maintain its current programs. The need to give current operations an implicit priority over new projects can present especially painful difficulties for archives, which generally exist in an environment of high, fixed costs (salaries and buildings, though "fixed" is a relative term) that cannot be easily pared to free money for new projects and limited opportunities for revenue growth. Let us nonetheless assume that, in addition, the society plans to improve or enhance its activities. As part of its overall planning process, let us further assume that three projects have been identified: automation of some office and archival functions, the acquisition of movable shelving, and the purchase of new furniture for the research room. Each of these projects can then be described as program items and given a priority rating. (See figure 11-4.)

Figure 11-4 Project Costs

Project	Costs 2001	Costs 2002	Total	Rank
Automation	$1,800	$1,800	$8,000	1
Shelving	6,000	4,000	10,000	2
Furniture	3,000	0	3,000	3

What do these project figures indicate? First, that management has selected automation over shelving and furniture as its highest priority. Also, that the furniture can be purchased in one fiscal year, with the shelving project paid for over two years. How many years will it take to finance the automation project? That is not apparent from the information supplied, though it will require funding after 2002, since $4,400 of its costs are not planned for either 2001 or 2002. By providing the full cost of the automation project, not just the costs to be incurred during the current budget/planning cycle, the repository has complied with the "full funding principle." This principle attempts to prevent managers from enticing resource allocators to approve what seem to be relatively inexpensive projects and then returning to ask for the additional equipment, personnel, or other resources needed to make that which has already been purchased work. An example of a "less than full funding" approach would be for an organization to obtain money to buy computers and only later indicate that it would perform more effectively as a local or wide area network. In the case of the automation project, it seems likely that the institution foresees future purchases of additional terminals or perhaps additional software, training, or maintenance.

Setting priorities does not necessarily mean an organization will expend its funds according to its priorities—an apparent contradiction. If the automation project is funded with grant money, the organization in all probability would not be permitted to shift the money to buy furniture. But if the Sample County Office of Cultural Affairs offered $1,500 to the historical society, how should this money be spent? It is unlikely that it could be used effectively for the automation project, an expenditure that seems to involve items costing $1,800. Could cheaper items be obtained? Possibly, but would they meet the organization's needs, and would they be compatible with later purchases? Could peripherals, for example, a modem or printer, be omitted? Again, this might be a possibility, but management would have to take a hard look at whether the purchased equipment would still meet management's objectives. In fact, shelving and furniture could be better uses for the windfall, because each would seem to better adapt to partial acquisition and implementation.

One other factor to be considered in "violating" one's own priorities is the manager's sense of which activities are most likely to get the support of resource allocators. Using the previous example, the manager may choose to use the windfall for furniture or shelving because such items are not likely to be highly attractive to higher management. They may be essential for the preservation of the collection, the appearance of the archives, or the comfort of researchers, but they are unlikely to excite the boss. Automation might, especially if the boss has made a commitment to the modernization of the archives. In the same way, foundations and other granting agencies are far more likely to respond to an automation proposal than to one for refurbishing old facilities and equipment.

Monitoring and Accounting

Financial control implies both accounting for the expenditure of resources and monitoring operations. The expenditure of resources is usually reported in financial terms. The use of personnel would, for example, be translated into payment of salary, facilitating analysis and comparison. Most techniques used to monitor operations also emphasize reporting, where possible, in quantitative terms. This preference for quantitative results is understandable in theory, but difficult to achieve in practice. In the archival environment, arriving at the number of feet of records processed or disposed of in a given period is easy, but how does one put a numerical value on the quality of assistance provided to a researcher? This problem will not be solved here, but it should be noted that excessive attention to quantity is possible, even to the point of adversely affecting the quality of an archives' operations. Better to admit some doubt about the measurable amount of work accomplished than to permit the archives' work to fall victim to a fetish for numbers.

The archival manager is not expected to be a licensed CPA, but some basic cost controls must be imposed, including explicit identification of those officials in an organization who have the authority to dispense funds. Archival managers need to understand that they bear ultimate responsibility for funds placed under their control. In most instances, managers act in a fiduciary capacity, with resources placed more in their trust than in their possession.

For most institutions, accounting is a relatively simple process of maintaining records of expenditures (receipts, invoices, etc.) and compiling that data periodically in a manner that permits the manager, auditors, or higher authorities to see that funds were disbursed in accordance with applicable policies and regulations and in pursuit of projects and objectives approved in the planning and budget processes.

For many institutions, *cash accounting,* familiar to everyone as the accounting procedure used with a checkbook, should be sufficient. Income is credited at the time it is received or made available for use, and costs are noted when bills are paid. A more complicated process, known as accrual accounting, may be required in larger repositories and in those that are part of larger operations, where *accrual accounting* is the norm.[3] An accrual system records income when it is earned by sales or services, even if this precedes actual receipt of the money owed. It accounts for expenses when they are incurred, even if payment takes place somewhat later. Accrual accounting distinguishes between *cash flow* and *funds flow,* a distinction most of us do not encounter handling our personal finances. Suppose an archives receives $1,000 a year for preservation supplies and early in the fiscal year, orders $100 of such items. At the moment the commitment is made, the institution's funds available for preservation are reduced to $900, even though no money has changed hands. Once the supplies are received, periodic financial statements would have to show this expenditure, even if the bill is not due for payment in that period. A flow of funds has taken place, though no cash flow will occur until the bill is paid.

Organizations should attempt to estimate their expenditures over the course of the fiscal year in quarterly or semiannual intervals. Whatever the interval used, managers should review their performance at the end of each period. Is expenditure meeting, exceeding, or falling short of target? Are variances planned and justifiable, or will they require reductions later in the year? The answers to questions such as these are essential pieces of management information.

---

3 To confuse the issue, many organizations use a mixed cash-accrual system. For more information, see Charles T. Horngren, et al., *Introduction to Financial Accounting,* 7th ed. (Upper Saddle River, N.J.: Prentice-Hall, 1999), or a similar introductory level accounting text.

Active Financial Management

As this discussion has suggested, financial management is far more complicated than simply preparing a budget and following it rigidly through an operating period. Circumstances change, and managers must be prepared to adapt to those changes. Some cost increases (overtime pay) can be controlled; others (a postal rate increase) cannot. The same uncertainty applies to revenue. In the case of the Sample County Historical Society, an increase in costs or a shortfall of revenue will require action on the part of management. Although little can be done with such items as salaries, early recognition of the problem might lead to cancellation of plans to attend a conference or perhaps to reduce spending on such items as supplies or postage.

What authority does the manager have to alter a budget, or to "reprogram funds"? Reprogramming rules and policies vary from organization to organization, so the best advice is to learn the policies of the institution. In many cases, a manager might have independent authority to reprogram within certain dollar limits without seeking approval from higher authority, with such approval required for larger amounts. Other organizations will, unfortunately, have more centralized controls that further limit or even eliminate independent reprogramming.

Financial planning and management can be a demanding and competitive arena. Texts on the subject are full of various ploys to enhance one's position, survive budget cuts, and gain the advantage over competitors. Language and metaphors drawn from sports and games (the shell game, the end run, the hidden-ball trick) and from warfare (divide and conquer) abound. Managers should expect that at some point they will come face-to-face with questions of legality and ethics. This manual can only suggest that managers need to know what is legal (meaning the regulations of a parent organization as well as civil statutes) and be alert to the ethical implications of their actions.

Conclusion

Effective, active financial management is an essential tool for the archival institution that hopes to survive, let alone prosper. An understanding of this tool can be a key to improving performance, planning for future needs, and impressing resource allocators with the effectiveness of the archival program. Used positively and aggressively, good financial management might even influence resource allocators to take a different view of the archivists they employ. In fact, a reputation for sound financial management may influence resource allocators to support the archival program in obtaining more funding or protecting funding during times of financial cutbacks.

Suggested Readings

A useful work from a related field is G. Edward Evans, et al., *Management Basics for Information Professionals,* which devotes a chapter (15) to fiscal management and contains references and suggested reading. Another helpful work is Robert Rachlin, ed., *Handbook of Budgeting,* 4th ed. (New York: John Wiley and Sons, Inc., 1999). This text brings together various aspects of budget preparation and presentation for both profit and nonprofit organizations. An earlier work, Robert D. Vintner and Rhea K. Kish, *Budgeting for Not-for-Profit Organizations* (New York: Free Press, 1984), provides useful information on the budgeting cycles and samples of forms that should be readily adaptable by a variety of institutions.

Chapter 12

Fund-Raising and Development

Financial planning is one of the most important skills that the archival manager must acquire and effectively use. The competition for resources both within an institution and from external funding sources is equally fierce. The successful manager must understand funding needs, determine whether internal or external funding (or a blend) is the most likely source, and then develop an effective strategy to achieve funding goals. This chapter will focus on those needs—programmatic, capital, or endowment—that exceed current budget levels and require fund-raising. Financial planning, funding sources, and the development program itself are integral to organizational success.

Archival Role

The manager must understand the archives' role within the parent organization's fund-raising and development structure. Most parent institutions, such as universities, museums, or libraries, will have a development program and staff in place to lead the effort to achieve the fund-raising goals and targets set by the institution. It is very important that any archival fund-raising effort be fully coordinated with the larger institution's programs and fit within the goals and objectives of the wider organization.

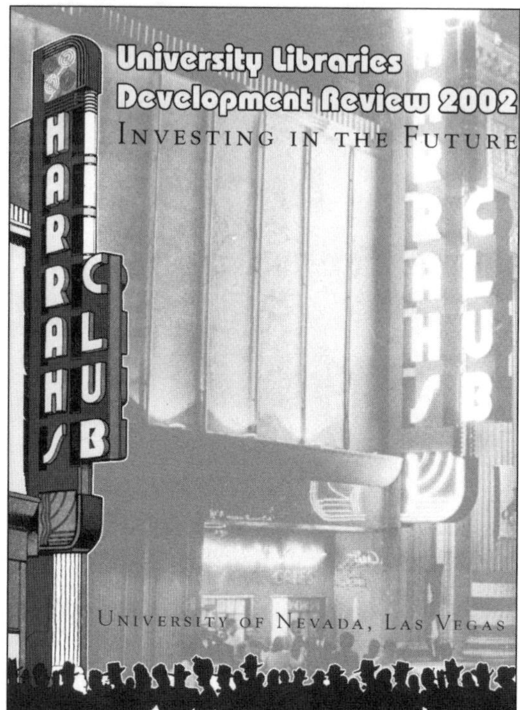

University Libraries
Development Review 2002
INVESTING IN THE FUTURE
HARRAH'S
CLUB
UNIVERSITY OF NEVADA, LAS VEGAS

Publications such as a development review can be very helpful for financial planning and fund-raising. They allow the institution to promote its activities to researchers, prospective donors, previous donors, and staff. UNIVERSITY OF NEVADA LAS VEGAS

Fund-raising is a time-consuming and challenging effort. The archival manager should first determine that program needs cannot be obtained through the usual budget process and that fund-raising is potentially the best vehicle for obtaining needed funding. If that is the case, then the archival manager should approach the development office with a detailed statement of need and options for beginning a campaign.

The parent institution may have an advisory board with fund-raising responsibilities already in place. If that is the case, the archival manager should work with the director of development and the board to begin analyzing the fund-raising need and the potential viability of the project. If there isn't an advisory board, or if it is not suitable to work with the board, the archival manager should seriously consider creating such a board to support the archives. This, of course, should be done with the concurrence and support of the parent institution's development director and senior management.

For major projects, the archival manager, the development director, and the advisory board should consider hiring a consultant to conduct a feasibility study to determine the viability of the proposed project. A consultant can objectively assess the fund-raising potential of the project and any impact that the campaign might have on other fund-raising efforts planned or underway.

The archives' can play an important role as a resource for the institution's fund-raising campaigns. Archival holdings most likely will contain documentation useful from both an informational and graphics point of view. Archival holdings can provide the historical context and factual basis needed for any effective campaign. Continually demonstrating the ongoing value of the archives to the institution is a task that the archival manager must constantly keep in mind. Posters, photographs, and textual documents can become integral parts of fund-raising campaigns, exhibits, and public information initiatives.

But the first step in any fund-raising effort begins with planning.

Planning

Fund-raising efforts grow naturally out of strategic and long-term planning. Defined missions, goals, and objectives are the cornerstones for determining funding priorities and strategies. When completed, planning yields a list of items for which funds are available and identifies those that cannot be accomplished at current funding levels.

Before approaching the institution for additional funding support, or considering going out to external sources via a fund-raising campaign, the archival manager should carefully review the project or program that requires additional support. This review should highlight and specify

1. Goals: What are the goals of the program? Is the intent to make archival collections more readily available? Is the program geared toward the conversion of collections? Is a new or remodeled facility required? Is a new exhibit or outreach effort planned? Such issues should be carefully thought out before proceeding further.
2. Activities: Based on the stated goals, what activities will be required to achieve those goals? This profile should include not only the specific steps needed to complete the program, but also a listing of personnel, equipment, space needs, and supplies.
3. Costs: When the activities have been defined, the archival manager should develop a rough estimate of the costs for the

> total project. This should not be an attempt to develop a finalized budget, but only a general estimate of the funds that are needed. With this information the archival manager can decide whether the project may be too large or too small for specific funding agencies.

At this point archival managers have several choices. They can return to the administration of their parent institution to advocate the need for additional funding, or they can immediately seek outside support. The former strategy is often successful and should be attempted before other funds are sought. Arguing for increased internal support is useful since it educates resource allocators to the needs and priorities of the archives. But if the latter strategy is required, immediate consultation with the development office should be initiated.

Seeking Internal Funding

Archival managers seeking funding for new programs should usually begin the search within their own institution before looking outward, unless, during the planning exercise, management has decided that fund-raising is the most appropriate funding vehicle. Preparing a budget proposal requires careful planning as well as a marshaling of support. Archival managers must familiarize themselves with available alternatives within the institution and match needs with funds. The archivist must be aware of the parent institution's budgetary structure. If funds are not available from the current operating budget, other sources might be sought. For example, some institutions retain capital reserves for constructing and remodeling facilities and purchasing capital equipment. Such reserves could be tapped for building renovations or the purchase of a new computer. Other institutions maintain discretionary and endowment funds. Some funds may be released with the approval of the parent institution's administration, others may be used only for specific purposes. Knowing the nature of these funds can be a valuable tool in seeking financial support.

The archival manager must marshal support from internal constituencies. Two groups with a vested interest in the repository are its donors and members of its advisory committee. Chapter 13 will discuss the need for archival managers to encourage support for the archives from different constituencies. Such support is an important ingredient in the success of every repository, but becomes critical when the archives has financial needs beyond its normal budget.

Seeking External Funding

Important programs often require full or partial support for which internal funding is not available. At such times, the archival manager must look beyond the parent institution for financial support. If the archives is part of a larger institution such as a university, a library, or a religious or charitable organization, the archivist should begin by meeting with the fund-raising or development officer. The archival manager can gain useful insights from the development officer's expertise and learn of possible sources of financial support. The archivist will also discover if the parent institution has imposed any restrictions on fund-raising. Some institutions require that all grants go through the development office, while others, such as religious agencies, may be unwilling to accept federal grants. If the parent institution does not have a development or fund-raising office, these issues should be discussed and cleared with the office responsible for seeking or receiving such outside funds. Whether or not the archives must channel requests through the development office, it should seek its assistance in reviewing grant proposals. Content, format, budget, and work plans should be examined. The development officer's experience can be crucial in presenting a proposal that meets the needs and timetable of a particular funding agency.

As archival managers begin to seek outside funding, they will become acquainted with grant officers and foundation administrators. Such individuals can provide helpful advice on sources of support when a proposal falls outside an agency's guidelines. The suggestions of grant officers can also assist applicants in revising or rethinking a proposal in its nascent stages. Archival managers should be aware, however, that fund-raising is a competitive field and that their initial ideas or concepts may require considerable revision before they find someone interested in funding their project. Both archival supporters and funding agency officials should be cultivated continually. Developing a network of contacts will provide informal responses to fund-raising ideas and offer leads to other sources of support.

Capital and Endowment Campaigns

Archival managers are often called upon to raise money for buildings, an endowment, or a new program, particularly when the parent institution is unable to provide full funding. Other activities that may require outside funding are building renovations, new facilities, or ongoing programs. Once the planning exercise is complete, and both program and funding needs are clear, the archival manager should attempt to discover whether it is possible to raise the amount of money that is required. Large fund-raising projects often require additional expertise or support and will undoubtedly involve the parent institution's development department and/or private companies or consultants who specialize in feasibility studies and in fund-raising itself.

The archivist should do considerable research before engaging a fund-raising firm. He or she should seek the names of companies from other agencies who have carried out building or endowment campaigns, research the services offered and the fees charged, and obtain the names of similar organizations that have used the firm's services for references. Fund-raising companies provide a range of support from advice to full responsibility for the complete campaign. Fees for their services will vary depending upon their involvement in the campaign and may range from a set fee to a percentage of the total funds raised.

Companies that carry out feasibility studies will research sources from which to raise the needed funds and identify their level of giving. Such a study may indicate the possibility of success or suggest the need to revise the funding goals and the resulting program.

Capital and endowment fund-raising are both difficult and time-consuming. Such projects should not be embarked upon lightly and should only begin after archival managers have the total involvement and support of the parent institution, the archives' governing board or advisory board, and the parent institution's development office.

Development offices and fund-raising firms will use annual giving campaigns or capital campaigns depending upon the nature of the project or program. An annual giving campaign usually involves a Friends Group or support organization for the archives whose members contribute an annual gift. Often members of these groups receive subscriptions to the archives' publications, discounts on items for sale, or other benefits commensurate with their annual gift. Capital campaigns are much larger enterprises that target a selection of potential donors, using individual solicitations and intensive follow-up to ensure that each donor has a satisfactory relationship with the archives.

In addition to individual donors, two significant funding sources are foundations, corporate or philanthropic, and government agencies on the federal, state, and local levels.

Foundations

Philanthropic giving, channeled through corporate and private foundations, provides millions of dollars each year in the form of grants to nonprofit and charitable organizations. Although they may seem to be the first place to seek funds, foundations should be approached only after thorough investigation. Foundations usually support specific types of programs and may restrict support to specific geographic locations. Some foundations may only give funds for medical research in the state of Delaware, while others limit their giving to educational programs in Milwaukee, Wisconsin. Such restrictions may be part of the guidelines originally established by the donor or may reflect the current policy of the foundation's board. Some large foundations change their program emphases over time to reflect current social needs or the board's composition or outlook.

Archival managers should begin their search for outside funds by first reviewing the foundations in their local community and those located within their state. Starting locally or regionally, the archival manager has a better chance of finding a foundation that might support a specific project. Some large foundations fund library and historical projects on a national basis, but they are scarce, and there is a great deal of competition for their funds.

The Foundation Center publishes *The Foundation Directory,* a list of foundations organized first by state and then alphabetically by name. Indexes include a state list, subdivided by city, and a subject index. Each listing provides financial data, purpose, and activities; application information; address and telephone number. Archival managers should know the foundation's general giving pattern but should also research the types of projects it has funded in recent years and the average size of grants awarded. This information is found in a database and computer printouts compiled by the Foundation Center library. The database can be searched for specific geographic areas or types of recipients such as libraries, archives, and historical programs. Such material can be used, without cost, at the Foundation Center library, its branches, or through major regional libraries. The center also provides many services to individual institutions on a fee basis. Copies of foundation annual reports also give such data and are available at the Foundation Center library or directly from individual foundations.

When a foundation has been identified as a possible supporter of archival programs, the manager should approach the foundation to discover its interest in providing support for specific programs. If the initial contact can be made by an archives advisory board member, an archives supporter, or someone in the parent institution's development office who is acquainted with the foundation staff or board, the chance of success improves. If it cannot, the archival manager should call or write the foundation, discussing the proposal in general terms and requesting guidelines and applications. If the foundation shows interest, the archival manager should begin establishing a relationship with the foundation staff and preparing a formal proposal.

Government Agencies

Some government agencies provide support for archives, libraries, and museums. Here again, the search for a likely funding source should begin at the local level and expand outward. A number of states have developed grant programs in the arts, history, or humanities. Some state archival agencies have begun offering grants to local archival programs with funding from either federal or state sources. Archival managers should discover whether such agencies exist in their state and research the types of programs eligible for funding and the average size of grant awards.

The federal government offers a number of grant programs of interest to archival managers. Some of the agencies providing grants include the National Historical Publications and Records Commission, the National Endowment for the Humanities, the National Endowment for the Arts, the Department of Education, the Institute of Museum and Library Services, and the National Science Foundation. Programs range from general operating support from the Institute of Museum and Library Services, to preservation grants from the National Endowment for the Humanities, to funds for the preservation of and increased access to American historical documentation, in its myriad forms and formats. (See figure 12-1.) Some grant-making organizations, such as the National Endowment for the Arts, provide grants only to nonprofit organizations incorporated under Section 501(c)(3) of the Internal Revenue Code.

The purposes of government grant programs are defined by law. Emphases change over time, however. A review of federal agencies will indicate whether a specific federal program provides funds for the type of program planned by the archives. If it does, the archival manager should write to the grant agency requesting additional information on grant programs and lists of grants that have been recently awarded. A follow-up call to discuss the proposal with a program officer is also advisable at this stage, and continued contacts are helpful at various stages of the grant-writing process.

Grant Applications

Archival managers should learn all they can about the funding agencies to which they are applying. They should request copies of application forms, guidelines, and instructions, and they should continue to review these during the application process to ensure that all of the

Figure 12-1 Federal Agencies Offering Grant Support

Department of Education
Office of Chief Financial Officer
Grants, Policy, and Oversight Office
7th and D Streets, SW
Washington, DC 20202
(202) 260-0172

Institute of Museum and Library Services
1100 Pennsylvania Avenue, NW, Room 609
Washington, DC 20506
(202) 606-8536

National Endowment for the Arts
1100 Pennsylvania Avenue, NW
Washington, DC 20506
(202) 606-5400

National Endowment for the Humanities
1100 Pennsylvania Avenue, NW
Washington, DC 20506
(202) 606-8400

National Historical Publications and Records Commission
National Archives and Records Administration
700 Pennsylvania Avenue, NW, Room 106
Washington, DC 20408
(202) 501-5600

National Science Foundation
4200 Wilson Boulevard
Room 405
Arlington, VA 22230
(703) 292-8210

funding agency's requirements are met. It may even be useful to develop a checklist of requisite tasks and deadlines. Archival managers must know their audience and make applications concise, realistic, and tailored to the purposes of the funding agency to which they are being sent. If an agency does not normally provide funds to archival programs, it may be necessary to include more detailed information about archival procedures or goals, either verbally or through the written application. Applicants should seek advice and response from the foundation or agency before and during the application process. If it is possible to visit and meet staff members, the archivist should do so. Some government agencies hold office hours at professional meetings, such as the annual meeting of the Society of American Archivists, offering an informal opportunity to discuss grant concepts or proposals in draft form. Applicants should not overlook archival colleagues as sources of information. Opinions should be sought about possible grant concepts. Finally, when an application has been drafted, a critical review by several professionals outside the archives can greatly improve a proposal. An outsider's perspective can reveal an application's lack of information, clarity, or logic.

Applications vary depending upon whether the archives is applying to a private foundation or a public agency. Some private foundations have a formal application form, while others ask only for a letter describing the project and the amount of money requested. In either event, applications to private foundations are likely to be shorter and require less time to complete because foundations tend to operate more informally than government agencies. Private foundations usually meet on a regular basis to review applications. Most meet quarterly, with larger ones meeting monthly and smaller ones sometimes meeting only annually or semiannually. Archival managers should schedule their work to meet application deadlines and response dates.

The government grant application process tends to be considerably more complicated. Applications generally require much more information and are more lengthy than those of private foundations. Each agency has a specific format and requires certain types of information. (See figure 12-2 for a sample grant proposal from the National Historical Publications and Records Commission.) Because of the time required, it is wise to discuss planned projects with agency staff

Figure 12-2 NHPRC Application (Example)

1. **Purpose and Goals of Project**
   The Center for the Study of Commerce requests a grant to arrange and describe 15 collections documenting the history of business and commerce in the United States. The primary goal of the project is to increase access to and use of records and to strengthen the Center's capacity to make available a significant body of records. The grant will allow us to arrange and describe 15 collections of personal papers and business records totaling 267 cubic feet, and create 15 finding aids and MARC:AMC records for loading into OCLC and RLIN.

2. **Significance and Relationship to NHPRC Goals and Objectives**
   This project relates to the NHPRC objective of increasing access to and use of records. The 15 collections span the years 1879–1987 and consist of records that have a broad importance to the study of the history of the United States. They will be of value to a broad range of users from scholars to the general public.

3. **Plan of Work**
   The duration of the project will be 18 months. The total amount of materials to be processed is 267 cubic feet. The Project Archivist will arrange and describe the records in accordance with national standards. The collections will be processed in priority order: the most important and fragile collections will be processed first. The collections will be surveyed and series and folder arrangements will be identified. Original order will be maintained whenever possible, duplicates will be weeded, and paper clips and staples will be removed. Records will be placed in appropriate acid-free folders and boxes, labeled, and stored in a secure and environmentally sound storage facility. Processing will proceed at an estimated rate of 10 hours per cubic foot and is expected to take 16 months to complete. Several of the collections are in a state of disorder, but most are in good condition. The remaining two months will be dedicated to completing the 15 finding aids, creating MARC:AMC records, loading records into OCLC and RLIN, posting the finding aids on the Center's Web site, and publicizing the completion of the project.

(continued)

Figure 12-2 continued

4. Products/Publications to Be Completed During Grant Period

The project will produce the following:

- 15 finding aids, one for each collection processed, in printed form and also encoded for use on the Center's Web site.
- 15 catalog entries prepared in marc:amc format and loaded into national bibliographic databases.
- Press releases and announcements will be prepared for online sites as well as for publications such as newsletters.

Project Narrative

Purpose and Goals of Project

This is a project to arrange and describe records that document the history of business and commerce in the United States, and particularly in New England and the Northeast. The 15 collections to be organized are a part of the Archives Department of the Center for the Study of Commerce acquired by donation. This project will increase access to and use of records in the area of American business history. Since 1989 when the Center formally established a historical records program with funding from foundations, our aim has been to enhance our ability to preserve the history of business and commerce and to ensure access to a broad clientele. Initial funding allowed us to organize our first archival acquisitions and we have succeeded in sustaining our program, adding collections, and developing into a fine repository. This project will continue to strengthen our institution and help us to make available a significant body of records.

The Center's archives is one of the principal research repositories in the area of business and commerce. Over the years the archives has evolved to meet the needs and demands of an ever-expanding constituency. It is open to the public and serves a diverse group of users from the surrounding area, across the United States, and from abroad. Its mission is to identify, collect, preserve, and make accessible information sources that document business and commerce in the United States.

(continued)

Figure 12-2 continued

Although archival collections were donated to the Center as early as 1983, we did not establish a formal archival program until 1989. Currently the holdings total over 2,700 cubic feet and include the records of large and small businesses, professional organizations, personal papers, and other collections. The Center's administration is fully committed to supporting this project and the future efforts of the archives. We now have a full-time archivist on staff who provides reference services, maintains collections, conducts donor outreach, and helps to supervise processing projects.

Significance of the Project and Use of the Records

The project aims to preserve and make accessible the documentary heritage of business and commerce in the United States. The Center is one of the few institutions that is systematically collecting these records and making them available. Usage of the archives has grown steadily over the years and currently averages 500-600 researchers a year. The archives maintains a log of all users of the collections as well as a more detailed user form with information about the topic people are researching. This information helps the staff of the archives determine which unprocessed collections are likely to be desired by researchers. These collections are then given priority for early processing. Past usage of the Center's collections reflects a great deal of diversity of people and purpose. The collections have been utilized for a wide variety of monographs and other books, exhibits, curriculum guides, television documentaries, special issues of newspapers, and other uses. In addition to users from the local area, researchers have come from other regions of the country and from abroad.

The Collections

The 15 collections we are aiming to organize span the years 1879–1987. They document key areas in the history of business and commerce and include the papers of individuals and the records of several businesses. The records contained in the collections are diverse and rich. There are ledgers, journals, lists of stockholders and stock certificates, employee

(continued)

Figure 12-2 continued

records, personal and business correspondence, blueprints, news clippings, inventories, scrapbooks, pamphlets and advertisements, and photographs. We expect that all of these collections, once processed, will be heavily utilized by scholars, students, and the general public seeking biographical historical documentation, and for educational purposes.

Condition of the Records

The condition of the records is good overall. Most were stored in people's homes or offices. Four collections are in very fragile condition, with brittle and deteriorating paper, due to having been stored in abandoned warehouses and other unsecured commercial properties. Several of the larger collections are in a state of disorder and will require extra time for processing. Half of the collections include photographs and negatives that are in good condition. There are some scrapbooks, which will require careful handling. Currently, all of the collections are housed in an area with adequate environmental and security controls.

Plan of Work

The goal of the project is to arrange and describe 15 collections of business records and personal papers ranging in size from one to 59 cubic feet. The total amount of material to be processed is 267 cubic feet. The project archivist will arrange and describe the records in accordance with national standards. The collections will be surveyed, and series and folder arrangements will be identified. Whenever possible original order will be maintained. Duplicates will be weeded and paper clips and staples will be removed. Once materials have been processed they will be housed in appropriate acid-free folders and boxes, labeled, and stored.

Processing will ideally proceed at the rate of ten hours per cubic foot. Several of the collections are in poor order and four are in extremely fragile condition. The most important and most fragile collections will be processed first. The processing portion of the project should be completed

(continued)

Figure 12-2 continued

in about 16 months. Two additional months will be utilized for preparation of finding aids, posting the finding aids on the Center's Web site, and publicizing the completion of the project. Finding aids will include a statement of provenance, biographical or organizational sketch, scope and content note, container lists, and a list of subject headings. The records will be open to the public on equal terms for everyone. We foresee few restrictions, except possibly for some more recent employee records that may be included in one of the collections. Descriptive information about the records will be entered into both OCLC and RLIN.

Staffing

Institutional Archivist (currently on staff) will serve as project director and will devote 25% of his time. Responsibilities include general project administration, hiring and supervising the project archivist, publicity, writing progress reports, and reviewing and editing the finding aids.

Project Archivist (to be hired) will serve as a full-time, grant-funded employee. Responsibilities include the arrangement and description of the collections, preparation of finding aids, and creation of worksheets for MARC:AMC records.

Cataloger (currently on staff) will commit 5% of her time to the project. Responsibilities include assisting in the preparation of the MARC:AMC worksheets, loading descriptive information into OCLC and RLIN, and preparing finding aids for posting on the Center's Web site.

Student Assistants (to be hired) will be hired by the Center to assist the Project Archivist with processing tasks such as removal of staples and paper clips, photocopying, and basic cleaning of documents.

(Courtesy of the National Historical Records and Publications Commission, National Archives and Records Administration)

before drafting a full application. Such discussion could indicate whether a proposal is competitive with other applications, or whether major changes should be made in the initial proposal. Grant staff may also be willing to review a proposal before submission, suggesting changes that will help it meet grant agency guidelines as well as make the project more effective.

Applicants must be realistic in drafting their proposals. Credibility is an important commodity with granting agencies, and an archives should not promise more than it is capable of producing. Application forms vary from agency to agency, but each should include the following types of information:

1. PURPOSE: The proposal must establish why the project is important and explain the benefits it will bring to the institution, its constituents and/or users, or to the archival community. This is one of the most critical issues that the proposal will address. The archival manager must make a good case for the project, indicating not only why it is important to the institution's development, but also how it fits into a larger archival context.
2. GOALS: The proposal must indicate what goals and objectives the institution plans to achieve in the course of the planned project. The goals and objectives should be part of the archives' larger planning process and will become a factor in the granting agency's evaluation of the grant proposal.
3. PLAN OF WORK AND TIMETABLE: To reach the project's goals, the proposal should list the tasks to be completed. A schedule should indicate completion dates for various tasks. If the proposal sets targets for the amount of material processed, surveyed, or appraised, it should provide evidence that these goals can be achieved based on institutional evidence or experience at other archival institutions.
4. STAFF: The proposal should list all staff members connected with the project, indicating the role they will play in achieving project goals. The application should also include a resume or curriculum vitae for each indicating their qualifications.
5. BUDGET: Each proposal should have a full budget listing expenses for personnel, personnel benefits, supplies, equip-

ment, travel, or other expenses connected with the project. Most granting agencies will require matching funds or cost sharing, and figures should be included for personnel overhead and indirect costs not paid by the grant.

Managing Grants

The receipt of a grant is the beginning, not the end, of the grant process. Too often, archival managers are not prepared to manage the grants once they have been received. Grants require a management process that parallels that of the full archival institution. This may entail the recruitment, selection, and supervision of additional staff, maintenance of budgets, and preparation of periodic reports. Sufficient time must be allotted for archival managers and repository staff to carry out these tasks if the grant program is to be successful.

Archival managers should carefully review reporting guidelines. Government grants require frequent written and financial reports, while foundations generally have fewer reporting guidelines. Weekly logs or reports of completed work will ease this task. Grant funds should be segregated in a separate account for ease of reporting. With a separate fund, it will be easier to track expenditures in different categories. Some agencies allow grant funds to be placed in interest-bearing accounts, while others do not. Guidelines on these matters should be carefully followed.

Recruitment of staff should follow the procedures outlined in the grant proposal. Government granting agencies may require a national search, while foundations may have no guidelines at all. Recruiting staff may be difficult because grant projects generally are completed within one or two years. This situation can be alleviated, however, if the salary level for grant personnel is at or above permanent staff levels. Grant personnel should become an integral part of the archives, participating in normal staff activities and receiving standard benefits. Careful selection, supervision, and nurturing will allow grant staff members to complete their assigned tasks on schedule.

Funding agencies judge archives not only on the basis of the value and creativity of the grants that are submitted, but also on the archives' ability to carry out successfully the tasks that it has proposed. Grant management plays an important role in ensuring that the program is completed on time and within the budget and should not be overlooked by archival managers.

Conclusion

The archival manager is responsible for ensuring that the archives has sufficient resources to achieve its goals. Financial support, though critical to success, is frequently inadequate. Through planning, financial analysis, and persuasion, archival managers can increase funding and expand archival opportunities for their institutions by using imagination, research, and resourcefulness. Fund-raising and development is a new arena for many archival managers. It is important to identify resources, such as written guides or handbooks on fund-raising and associations of fund-raising and development professionals, to better understand the fundamentals of this professional endeavor.

Suggested Readings

An excellent work for archivists and managers is Elsie Freeman Finch, ed., *Advocating Archives: An Introduction to Public Relations for Archivists* (Metuchen, N.J. and London: The Society of American Archivists and Scarecrow Press, 1994), which deals with fund-raising and public relations.

Useful works from related fields include Victoria Steele and Stephen D. Elder, *Becoming a Fundraiser: The Principles and Practice of Library Development* (Chicago: American Library Association, 2000); and Adam Daniel Corson-Finnerty and Laura Blanchard, *Fundraising and Friend-raising on the Web* (Chicago: American Library Association, 1998).

There are several valuable guides to funding sources. The Foundation Center in New York publishes the *Foundation Directory,* the *National Directory of Corporate Giving,* the *Guide to U.S. Foundations, Their Trustees, Officers, and Donors,* and the *National Guide to Funding for Libraries and Information Sources.* These works provide definitive information to nonprofit organizations on private and community grant-making foundations, along with contact information and sample grant applications.

CHAPTER 13

Public Relations

Public relations refers to the communication or dialogue about its services and goals that an archives has with individuals or groups inside and outside its institutional setting. Public relations is an integral part of management and must be a deliberate effort included in the long-range planning process.

Communication must be part of a well-planned program designed to explain the archives' mission and involve people in its program. It can take a variety of forms: up-to-date and informative Web sites, press releases, conversations between researchers and reference archivists, or annual reports prepared for the archives' parent institution, for example. Public relations can also include special events designed to invite specific groups to ceremonial openings or other events.

Public relations must begin with a clear understanding of the archives' mission and its various publics. In developing a public relations program, an archival manager must distinguish between public relations, public programs, and outreach. Public relations is concerned with communication between the archives and its public in whatever form that communication may take. Public programs and outreach are educational and marketing tools that provide products and services to varied audiences. However, such efforts should fall under the overall rubric of public relations so that such efforts foster a better understanding of the archives and its mission.

Archival Image

One of the purposes of archival public relations programs is the establishment of an appropriate image. Archivists must convince their public and their employers that their work is of significant value to the parent institution. According to studies done by the Society of American Archivists, archivists are often seen as helpful, but not vital, to the overall institutional mission. Is it any wonder then, that when an institutional budget crunch comes, or new management is looking for ways to improve profits, that the archives is often one of the first departments to be cut?

The image that archivists want to project to employers, researchers, and the public will depend to some degree upon whether the program is an institutional archives or a manuscripts repository. Whatever the situation, archivists should strive to make clear that they provide a fast and dynamic service, that they have sources that no one else can provide, and that they are a department that the institution cannot do without. This is a tall order, but archivists who provide these services and use appropriate public relations techniques can work to achieve this goal.

Developing Constituencies

Successful archival programs develop large and loyal constituencies, groups or people with vested interests in the archives. These may be people who supervise the archives program, approve its budget, sit on its advisory board, use its holdings, read its newsletter, donate material to its collection, or think that having an archives is worthwhile. Their support may develop for emotional or practical reasons.

Archivists must begin by developing a plan for reaching those within their own organization, whether the repository is part of a business, university, state government, or nonprofit agency. An internal public relations program can take on many different faces, but whatever is envisaged should achieve the goal of making the archives an integral part of its parent organization.

Efforts may include assisting the public relations department by providing information, photographs, or other materials; writing articles for in-house and public consumption; providing information to the personnel department for new staff orientation; and developing exhibits or other projects that publicize the value and importance of the archives. Highlighting recently acquired collections or newly opened materials is also important. If well done, these internal efforts cultivate a large and growing group of archival supporters who better understand the mission of the archives. Whatever the level of interest or involvement, administrators and staff of the parent institution must have a positive image of the program. And they will, if the exhibits they see are professional and engaging, if the reference service they receive is complete, if collections are processed thoroughly and efficiently, or if they hear about the archives in a positive way from someone who has had contact with it. In these examples, the archives is cultivating individuals who are more likely to support its future endeavors. Success may not assure that the archives will achieve all its goals or get more funding, but failure to communicate is likely to lead to an unappreciated and underfunded program.

In addition to developing internal support from their parent institutions, many archives must develop outside constituencies. Public interest and support for the archival program is valuable for a number of reasons. First and foremost, good public relations will assist the archives in developing financial support. Second, being a vital community resource or valued by members of the public as a respected cultural center will assist the archives in developing its collections and acquiring useful material. Third, public interest should increase use of the archives' collections.

The emphasis on internal versus external constituencies will vary depending upon the type of archival institution. An institutional or business archives will focus its primary efforts on developing internal constituencies because most of its funding comes from its parent institution. A manuscript repository, on the other hand, must develop external constituencies that see the value of its mission and provide moral and financial support. A state archives must balance an internal constituency of government employees with the tax-paying public.

One of the goals of the archival manager should be to tailor the public relations program to the interests of various constituencies, strengthening the bonds of support between them and the archival

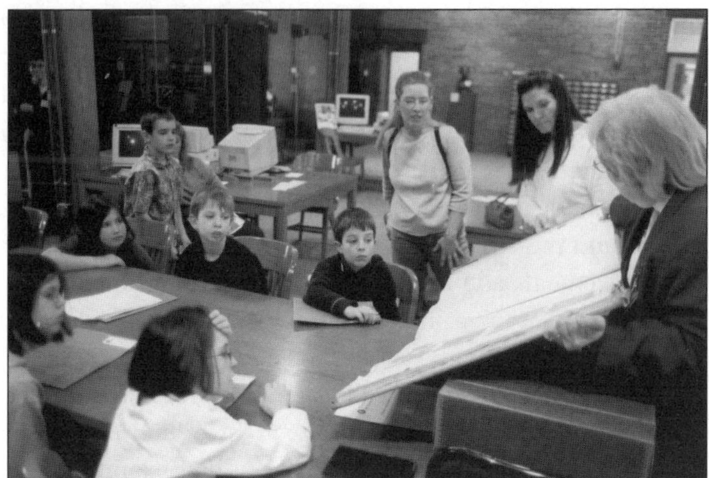

Public relations programs often involve introducing archival materials to school-age children. HISTORICAL SOCIETY OF WESTERN PENNSYLVANIA

program. This will not be an easy task because each group views the archives from a totally different perspective. Nonetheless, it is worth pursuing. If successful, the manager will know where to turn when the archives needs financial, institutional, or other support. The ability to draw on people with a vested interest in the program is a strong advantage.

Planning a Public Relations Program

In developing a public relations program, the archival manager should use the planning guidelines outlined in chapter 5. Plans should evolve from the mission statement that defines not only program goals but the constituencies for which the archives is responsible. Two lists should be compiled: one will include current constituents, evaluating whether their needs are being met. The second list should identify groups that are currently not being served, but that could be useful to the institution. A variety of communication tools could be considered as ways to approach these groups—open houses, specific programs, lectures, films, exhibits, press releases, newsletters, listservs, e-mail lists, and fax lists.

Planning should begin with market research to discover the constituencies that the archives should reach. After constituencies are identified, managers need further research to identify consumer needs and to develop a range of programs to meet them. Once this preliminary work is complete, the archivist should develop goals, objectives, and activities for an overall public relations agenda that includes an evaluation component to ensure that the programs are meeting institutional and public needs.

Public Relations Staff

The manager must first decide who will have overall responsibility for public relations. Public relations work requires judgment skills, in addition to strong writing skills and interpersonal relations. The person responsible should be carefully selected with these factors in mind. Only the very largest archives will be able to assign someone to carry out public relations responsibilities on a full-time basis. In most institutions, public relations naturally falls within the archival manager's responsibility. However, given the importance of this function, other alternatives should be considered. Staff members with skills or experience in this area could be given this task as one of their responsibilities. Another possibility is the appointment of an experienced volunteer as the public relations representative.

Whoever is responsible should work closely with the parent institution's public relations department or officer. The archives must coordinate its public relations effort with that of the parent institution, building on the success of ongoing programs while not interfering with established media or other relationships. At the same time, the archives should take advantage of the public relations department's expertise and its contacts outside the institutional setting.

Developing a Good Public Relations Attitude

To develop a good program, an archives must take public relations seriously. Public relations cannot, however, operate in a vacuum. A public relations program is only as good as the program it is publicizing. In business, excellent advertising has a difficult time selling a poorly designed or poorly manufactured product, and a poor archival program will meet the same fate. Standards must also be set for the material produced by the institution. Guidelines for writing and design should be established to govern the development of new publications prepared for public relations use.

Archival public relations programs should begin by ensuring that the services they offer are of high quality. Staff must know that the work they do is important and has an impact on those who come into contact with the archives. A pleasant, well-designed research room, knowledgeable staff with a welcoming demeanor, and easily accessible and usable finding aids send a positive signal to users of the resources. Whether assisting researchers, leading tours, or giving speeches, staff must be encouraged to behave in a friendly, courteous, and professional manner. All staff members must understand how each of them can personally aid a public relations effort. Frequent in-house training programs can go a long way in furthering this goal.

Marketing Archival Services

Public relations reaches a public that has little initial interest or information about archives. Few people have any experience using archives and must be educated to the value of both the collections and services. In addition, archivists must overcome a built-in reticence on the part of their users. Because relatively few people use archives and have only a vague notion of their value or content, their fear of the unknown must be overcome. Archives must be easily accessible and provide information that people need and can readily use. Marketing techniques used by repositories must emphasize such user-friendliness. Archivists must look at their procedures and collections from a user's viewpoint if they are to sell their product effectively.

If institutional archives are to market their programs successfully, they must carefully examine their institutional environment. Who are the resource allocators that must be moved to support the archives, and what is the most effective manner to reach them? Who

Promotional brochures are an easy and inexpensive way of providing collection and institutional information to researchers and donors. City of Dallas Municipal Archives, City Secretaries Office, City of Dallas

uses archival services? Who could use archival services, but does not? The archives must communicate with all of these audiences if it is to gain their support. Archival managers must be able to communicate the goal and mission of the institution to the general public and to the media. They must be able to translate their own institutional culture, its vocabulary, and methodology and to plan the outreach program to fit a specific setting. Such reviews should include all programs: publications, donor relations, exhibitions, or records management.

Manuscript repositories must approach this situation in a similar fashion. However, their task is more complicated because their resource allocators and intended audience are likely to be less specific and more diverse. Public relations efforts may require using one vocabulary and methodology with one audience and one quite different with another. While this may make manuscript administrators' tasks more difficult, it should not deter them from designing specific public relations programs for particular audiences.

Market research can be carried out in a number of ways. One method is through oral or written surveys. Surveys can be designed to study the needs of researchers or people using other services such as records management. To be effective, questions must be open ended and provide an opportunity to criticize or offer useful suggestions: How could service be improved? Was the system of finding aids easily understandable? Were records manuals useful? Was the information that was needed readily accessible? The surveys could be disseminated through the listservs of various constituencies.

If the archives is producing a brochure to publicize its services, it should decide to whom it will be directed. To ensure that the brochure is effective, the archival manager could select a focus group to review it during the writing and design phases. Participants in the test market can respond from their specific perspectives to ensure that the brochure communicates with the audience it is designed to reach. All archival public relations programs should have a market research component and require continuing feedback so that they meet audience needs.

Targeting Audiences

When developing a public relations message, the archives must carefully decide which audiences it wishes to reach and the methods that will most effectively communicate with those particular groups. For example, a brochure designed for fund-raising will probably look quite different from one designed to introduce researchers to an archives' collections and services. Similarly, articles written for the parent institution's publications can assume certain levels of knowledge that would be unwise in a public press release. Archival managers must develop a well-designed plan to reach each particular group. Such a plan must take into account the audience, the message, and the medium used to convey the message.

Since archives are usually short of both staff and money, a great temptation exists to develop public relations efforts that send one message to all audiences. Although this approach may be better than sending no message at all, the public relations program will be more effective if it can tailor its message to specific audiences.

Press Releases

To extend its message beyond those people who visit, the archives must make its presence known to the wider community. Effective use of the institution's Web site, newspapers, radio, and television are important means of reaching beyond the archives. Press releases are a proven means of distributing information to the media. Press releases can announce major donations, the opening of a new collection, lectures or exhibitions open to the public, and instructional classes, or they can provide general information or historical background about current events.

Press releases generally follow a standard format. They should be typed and double spaced and answer who?, what?, where?, when?, and why? (See figure 13-1.) The press release should be clear and concise. It should be positive and encourage people to participate in whatever type of program is being publicized. If funds are available, the archives should send one or more accompanying photographs illustrating the release, since this may encourage the newspaper to print the article. The name, address, and telephone number of the archives should be included along with the name of the person who can provide additional information about the event.

Good Media Relations

Press releases may provide information to the media, but they will not ensure that the message is distributed. Newspapers, radio, and television are inundated by press releases and must select those that they feel are of the greatest interest to their audience. If the message is to reach the public, archival managers or the responsible staff must develop a close working relationship with the media. They need to identify who covers historical or cultural organizations and attempt to become better acquainted with them. Providing reporters with general information about the archival program and inviting them to visit the archives will help them to understand the archives' mission and to place future press releases into an appropriate context. The archives can offer to provide additional background information

Figure 13-1 Press Release

National Archives

Washington, DC 20408

NEWS RELEASE

FOR IMMEDIATE RELEASE October 16, 2000

National Archives Releases 420 Hours of Additional Nixon White House Tape Recorded Conversations

WHAT: The National Archives and Records Administration (NARA) will open approximately 420 hours of White House tape recordings from the Nixon Presidency. The 4140 conversations were recorded at the White House from August 1971 to December 1971, and are the second of five chronological segments of conversations to be released. These tape segments are reproduced on 650 cassettes. In accordance with the Presidential Recordings and Materials Preservation Act of 1974 and its implementing regulations, the National Archives have designated 89 hours as personal and returnable to the Nixon Estate. Nine hours are restricted for national security, as provided for in Executive Order 12958. One hour is restricted for invasion of privacy, three hours as unintelligible, and four hours as non-historical.

The tapes cover a wide variety of domestic and foreign topics relating to international crises and initiatives; and domestic issues, such as the economy and political appointments. Topics of interest include:

1. The International Monetary System and the US Economy: There are several key policy discussions between the President, members of the

(continued)

Figure 13-1 continued

White House staff, senior administration officials, business and labor leaders, and foreign government officials. There are substantial discussions about the US decision to end the Gold Standard and allow the dollar to "free float." There are also discussions about the President's New Economic Policy, which provided for a wage and price freeze, a repeal of excise taxes, federal spending cuts, imports surcharges, and tax reforms.

2. The President's Trip to the People's Republic of China: There are many discussions throughout this period about the President's forthcoming trip to the PRC in February, 1972. They include logistical details and arrangements, media and press coverage, possible itineraries, public relations efforts, agenda proposals, and discussion topics for meetings with PRC leaders.

3. Supreme Court Appointments following the resignation of Justices Black and Harlan: There are detailed discussions between the President, members of the White House staff, Attorney General John Mitchell, Members of Congress, Governors, and other leaders. They discuss and evaluate several possible candidates and recent Supreme Court rulings (e.g. busing), the President's judicial philosophy, and the President's efforts to appoint a woman to the Supreme Court.

4. United Nations Vote to expel Taiwan from the UN General Assembly: There are several discussions between the President, members of the White House staff, Secretary of State William Rogers, US Ambassador to the UN George Bush, Members of Congress, and foreign leaders, detailing US efforts to prevent Taiwan's expulsion. There are also many conversations following the vote complaining about the UN delegates behavior, US reaction and US public relations efforts.

(continued)

Figure 13-1 continued

At the opening, the National Archives will also release corresponding portions of a tape log that includes the date, time, location, outline of conversations, and names of participants that will help locate conversations. Because this portion of the log contains 8,000 pages, researchers are encouraged to use the electronic version in CD-ROM, which can be accessed in Word and WordPerfect 6.1 formats.

WHEN: 9 A.M. Thursday, October 26, 2000.

WHERE: National Archives at College Park, 860 I Adelphi Road. Lecture Rooms D & E.

IMPORTANT INFORMATION: To assist researchers in locating conversations on the tapes, a free finding aid on disc in WordPerfect 6.1 and Word format will be available on Monday, October 23, at 9 A.M. in Room G-5 at the National Archives Building on Pennsylvania Avenue, between 7th and 9th Streets, NW. Beginning on Tuesday, October 24, the discs may be obtained from the Nixon Project staff at the National Archives at College Park by calling 301-713-6950.

All researchers must have a current National Archives researchers card. Clean research room rules will apply. No recording or transmission devices, of any kind, will be allowed in the research room. Laptop computers and stenographs will be allowed.

In accordance with NARA regulations, these tape segments may not be reproduced. The National Archives and Records Administration will revoke privileges for anybody who attempts to record these materials. In addition, all members of the organization with which he or she is affiliated will lose privileges for all future openings as well.

****

For press information, call the National Archives Public Affairs staff at 301-713-6000.

01-03

(Courtesy of the National Archives and Records Administration)

about particular stories or current events. By cultivating reporters, the archives increases the likelihood that its stories receive adequate coverage and makes it more probable that the reporters themselves will initiate requests to do feature stories or articles. Creating special opportunities for the media, including open houses, openings of collections, and so on, can be an extremely effective tool in helping to educate the press about archives and holdings.

Electronic and Other Media

Newspapers are one form of communicating information about the archival program, but archivists must look beyond this medium. Both radio and television offer useful avenues of communication. Scripted radio public service announcements read over the air can be very effective in getting the word out for free. The most popular formats are ten-, fifteen-, and thirty-second announcements. Writers should be concise and choose words carefully. Talk radio stations in many areas increasingly seek information on a variety of topics and can increase public knowledge through the use of the talk-back format. Cable television offers another avenue to publicize events and archival collections, and in many cases, time is available for the asking.

Archivists should take advantage of the lower cost and increasing availability of video presentations. With careful planning, videotapes can become another useful public relations tool. With audiences accustomed to receiving information primarily through television, archivists must develop means of communicating with them. Videotapes can be prepared for use on television, with small groups, or for use by individuals in their own homes. A section of the institution's Web site should be reserved for public affairs. It could be called "media desk" and include press releases, background materials on specific collections, fact sheets about the institution, scanned photos of the stacks and the research room, and photos of the collections that are being highlighted.

Archival Publications

To meet the specific needs of its different clienteles, the archives must develop publications to communicate its services and activities. Published brochures can be specially designed to market particular programs. One all-purpose brochure may meet the needs of small institutions, while large institutions should develop specialized brochures to inform researchers about archival services, encourage and inform potential donors of archival materials, publicize archival publications, or inform users of specialized services such as records management.

In drafting an all-purpose brochure designed for a number of uses, the archives must carefully consider its audiences and include information to meet all of their needs. By considering the differing needs of donors and researchers, the archives can create a relatively low-cost, effective tool that promotes its services. A brochure usually includes the archives' mission statement, address, telephone number, hours, and a map. It should be simply worded, avoiding technical language. It should be attractively designed and contain as many photographs and illustrations as the archives can afford. The brochure can be easily distributed by enclosing it in reference replies and letters requesting donations, including it as a newsletter insert, giving it to institutional employees with their payroll checks, sending it by special mailings to other cultural or historical organizations in the same geographical area, and placing it in brochure racks at the chamber of commerce, the public library, or other public places.

Newsletters

A newsletter can meet a number of informational needs. It can inform people of archival activities, provide dates for upcoming events, give news about new collections or collection openings, and provide historical or biographical articles. Its content must be designed for the intended audience: employees of the archives' parent institution or a more general audience including donors, users, and interested members of the public. (See figure 13-2.) Newsletters with a professional, glossy look can be produced using desktop publishing. They can be

Figure 13-2 Newsletter Article

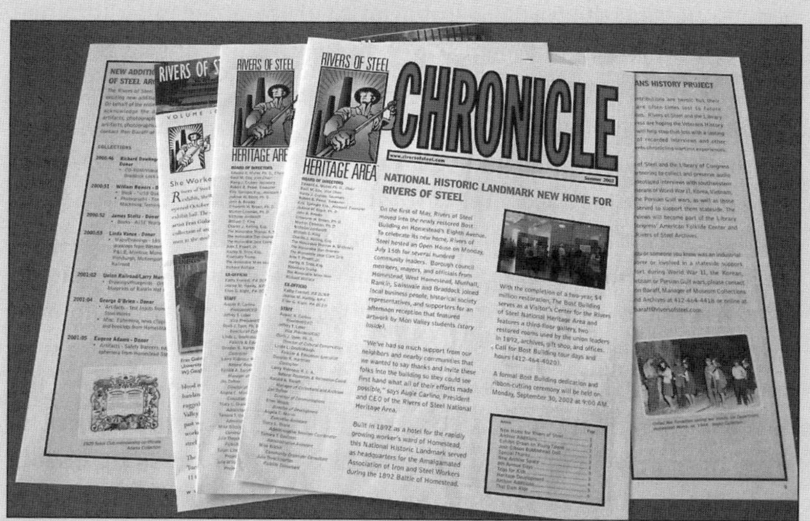

A newsletter describing holdings, activities, and acquisitions is one way an archives can keep in touch with donors and others interested in its collections.
COURTESY RIVERS OF STEEL NATIONAL HERITAGE AREA ARCHIVES

distributed in hard copy through the mail and can be posted on the Web site. Newsletters should be prepared and issued in close coordination with the public relations department or officer of the parent institution. Also, the archives can encourage other institutions or organizations to link their Web sites with that of the archives, thus increasing the potential reach of the public relations program.

Published Reports

A written annual report is yet another method of "communicating the archives' story," although it is often overlooked as a public relations tool by archival managers. An annual report can be aimed at a number of different audiences depending upon the archives' institutional affiliation. It can be strictly an internal document to show a parent organization the archives' current status, achievements, and future needs. An annual report, however, can also be an important tool for communicating the role and importance of the archives to administrators who have the archives as part of their responsibility. It should be attractive, brief, and distributed as widely as possible within the institutional hierarchy and to peers in other departments.

The annual report should be closely tied to the archives' long-range or strategic plan, and it should provide a means of measuring progress and revising the plan in view of institutional successes or failures. It should include statistical measurements of activities in which the archives is engaged. But it can also include anecdotal information, showing the impact of research in archives. By providing such information on a long-term basis, the archives can document such trends as reference use or acquisition and communicate needs to a variety of constituencies.

Publishing a brief, illustrated annual report intended for a wider audience is another useful public relations tool. A report designed for nonspecialists should be general and nontechnical in content. It should highlight the value of the archives through photographs, illustrations, and graphs that make archival functions understandable to the layperson. A successful report should encourage archival use by creating archival pride.

Conclusion

The list of possible public relations programs and activities is nearly endless, restrained only by the imagination and budget of the archivist. Clearly, not every activity mentioned in this chapter will be carried out by every archives. Archival managers, however, should plan an ongoing public relations program to help meet the archives' overall goals.

Public relations is critical in developing support for the archival program. With the information overload felt by individuals in modern society, people will not go out of their way to learn about new programs or new ideas. Because archives are not thoroughly understood, archivists have an even greater challenge, which requires an even greater effort than that of fellow professionals in cultural agencies such as libraries and museums. Information about archives must be brought to people in a familiar and understandable way. Failure to build support for the archives through a public relations program may lead not only to a lack of funding, but also to the demise of the program itself. Successful archival managers must find ways for their programs not only to survive, but also to prosper, and this can only be done through a planned and thorough public relations program.

Suggested Readings

An excellent work for archivists and managers is Elsie Freeman Finch, ed., *Advocating Archives: An Introduction to Public Relations for Archivists* which deals with public relations as well as with fund-raising. Many useful ideas, sample forms, and illustrations give the archival manager tools to use.

Other useful archival publications, though somewhat dated, include Ann E. Pederson, ed., *Keeping Archives* (Sydney, Australia: Australian Society of Archivists, 1987), 313–54; and Maygene Daniels and Timothy Walch, eds., *A Modern Archives Reader* (Washington, D.C.: National Archives and Records Service, 1984), which puts public programs into a management context (chapter 8).

Management Literature, Web Sites, and Professional Associations

The following essay provides an introduction to management literature and to a wide variety of professional associations. Briefly, professional associations range from academic organizations dealing with theoretical issues with little immediate impact on the working manager to those with a more practical mission. Not surprisingly, the periodical literature reflects this spectrum.

Archival and Related Associations

Professional associations within the archives, records-management, and library worlds tend to focus on what this manual has referred to as "technical management" rather than institutional management; that is, they are more concerned with the care of records and other materials than with the acquisition and use of resources. Nevertheless, these organizations recognize institutional management as a valid professional concern and sponsor journals and other publications, as well as conferences and workshops, pertaining to management and related topics. A partial list of such organizations follows.

The Society of American Archivists (SAA)
527 Well Street, 5th Floor
Chicago, IL 60607-3922
http://www.archivists.org

A directory of regional archival organizations is available on the SAA Web site at http://www.archivists.org/assoc-orgs/directory/index.asp.

Within SAA, the focal point for management issues is the Archives Management Roundtable, which, among other activities, publishes a newsletter containing book reviews and other features of interest to the archival manager.

National Association of Government Archivists and Records Administrators (NAGARA)
48 Howard Street
Albany, NY 12207
http://www.nagara.gov

ARMA International
13725 W. 109th Street
Suite 101
Lenexa, KS 66215
http://www.arma.org

American Association for State and Local History (AASLH)
172 Second Avenue, North, Suite 103
Nashville, TN 37201
http://www.aaslh.org

American Association of Museums (AAM)
1575 "I" Street, N.W., Suite 400
Washington, DC 20005
http://www.aam-us.org

American Library Association (ALA)
50 E. Huron Street
Chicago, IL 60611
http://www.ala.org

Special Libraries Association (SLA)
1700 Eighteenth Street, N.W.
Washington, DC 20009
http://www.sla.org

The Association for Information and Image Management (AIIM)
1100 Wayne Ave., Suite 1100
Silver Spring, MD 20910
http://www.aiim.org

Society for Information Management (SIM)
401 N. Michigan Avenue
Chicago, IL 60611
http://www.simnet.org

Professional Management Associations

The Encyclopedia of Associations (Farmington Hills, MI: Thomson Gale, 2004) lists over 23,000 national and international organizations, with several thousands of these devoted in some way to business, management, or the management of various technologies. Those noted below are but a sample.

Academy of Management (P.O. Box 3020, Briarcliff Manor, NY 10510-3020), http://www.aom@pace.edu. Membership in the academy includes academic professionals in business, management science, and related disciplines, as well as corporate executives selected on the basis of their contributions to management literature. The academy publishes the *Academy of Management Review*, with a strong theoretical and conceptual thrust, and the *Academy of Management Journal*, which attempts to put some emphasis on applications.

American Management Association (1601 Broadway, New York, NY 10019-7420), http://www.amanet.org/index.htm. This organization is very active in publishing and promoting workshops and conferences. AMA's focus is on the working manager, rather than on the academic pursuit of management science. AMA directs many of its efforts specifically at the professional-turned-manager.

American Society for Public Administration (Suite 700, 1120 "G" Street, N.W., Washington, DC 20005), http://www.aspanet.org. While many of the groups described here offer programs and literature of use to managers in both the for-profit and nonprofit sectors, ASPA focuses on the latter. In fact, ASPA has been an important factor in the development of professional standards and educational programs in the field of public administration.

American Society for Training and Development (1640 King Street, P.O. Box 1443, Alexandria, VA 22313), http://www.astd.org. The ASTD provides extensive information about resources available to managers for the development and training of staff for personnel administration and for managers themselves.

Association for Information and Image Management (1100 Wayne Avenue, Suite 101, Silver Spring, MD 20910), http://www.aiim.org. Organized in the 1930s as the National Microfilm Association, AIIM later evolved into the National Micrographics Association to encompass changes in microform techniques. Its latest transformation results from the advent of optical/digital storage devices. AIIM is an aggressive promoter of the combined meeting and trade show, complete with multitrack workshops on techniques and applications.

Center for Creative Leadership (One Leadership Place, P.O. Box 26300, Greensboro, NC 27438), http://www.ccl.org. The mission of the center is to advance the understanding, practice, and development of leadership in all sectors of society. It offers scholarship programs and organizational intervention with a special commitment to developing leadership in the nonprofit and educational sectors.

Project Management Institute (Four Campus Boulevard, Newtown Square, PA 19073), http://www.pmi.org. This is the world's leading nonprofit professional management association. The PMI offers numerous products and services explained on its Web site.

Society for Advancement of Management (SAM International Office, Texas A&M University, College of Business, 6300 Ocean Drive, FC 111, Corpus Christi, TX 78412), http://www.cob.tamucc.edu/sam. Though retaining academic ties, SAM is directed toward practical applications and runs an active program of workshops and conferences directed toward the needs of the working manager.

Periodical Literature

Since management for the information professional today encompasses both traditional managerial topics (personnel, finance, etc.) and the management of technology, journals on both are noted below.

Harvard Business Review. *HBR* remains a useful publication for several reasons, among them, its broad range of topics and a continuing editorial emphasis on the writing ability of its contributors. *HBR* achieves a comfortable balance between corporate, public, and academic contributors and topics.

Supervisory Management. Published by the American Management Association, this journal emphasizes brief, popularized articles focusing primarily on supervisory issues. A fairly entertaining publication, it runs case-study features in which readers are invited to submit their opinions for publication in a later issue.

Public Administration Review. Published by the American Society for Public Administration, *PAR* has long been an important source in its field. Public administration has encountered many of the same problems confronted by the archival profession, such as education, the need for research, and so on, and archivists might find the literature on these issues of great interest.

SAM Advanced Management Journal. Somewhat more focused than *HBR*, with emphasis on improving management techniques, the Society for the Advancement of Management's *Advanced Management Journal* frequently builds its issues around a single topic. Recent numbers have included such themes as "Employee Development and Productivity" and "Strategic Planning and Training."

Other Periodical Sources. Numerous periodicals are devoted to information management and technology. Some useful examples include the *Information Management Journal,* the *Journal of Knowledge Management, Records Management Quarterly,* and the *American Archivist.*

Reference Works

Readers should consult the suggested readings following each chapter and the occasional bibliographic footnotes.

In addition, several reference works are useful for the archival manager. The American Management Association's *Management Handbook,* edited by John J. Hampton, 3rd edition (New York: AMA, 1994) is a detailed manual covering every aspect of management tasks and responsibilities. Most helpful are the numerous sample forms needed by managers to perform their daily work. Three of the *Harvard Business Review*'s compilations of articles are particularly relevant: *On Management* (New York: Harper and Row, 1995); *On Human Relations* (New York: Harper and Press, 1979); and *On Effective Communication* (Cambridge, Mass.: Harvard Business Review Paperback, 1999). These editions bring together the most stimulating and useful articles around core management issues. G. Edward Evans, et al., *Management Basics for Information Professionals* is an extremely thorough exposition on every aspect of managing an information enterprise. While oriented toward libraries, almost all the material is relevant to the archival setting. Charts, graphs, and illustrations are potentially useful for the harried archival manager who doesn't have time to reinvent the wheel.

Books by management guru Tom Peters are always stimulating. Among the most noteworthy is *In Search of Excellence: Lessons from America's Best-run Companies* (New York: Harper and Row, 1982). Peter Senge has written or co-authored several notable texts about organizational transformation. These include *The Fifth Discipline: The Art and Practice of the Learning Organization* (New York: Doubleday/Currency, 1990), and *The Fifth Discipline Fieldbook: Strategies and Tools for Building a Learning Organization* (New York: Doubleday/Currency, 1994).

Concluding Note

In concluding this manual, I hope that more than anything else I have conveyed the excitement, challenges, and satisfaction that can come from a management job well done. Management provides the archival practitioner with the opportunity to gain a broader perspective and accomplish tasks that can potentially benefit the archival enterprise for years to come. The greatest satisfaction can come from mentoring and aiding staff members in their professional development, perhaps the greatest long-term service to the organization that the manager can provide.

Management knowledge and skills can get rusty fairly quickly in the dynamic environment in which archival managers operate. Learning for managers must be lifelong, and it requires a sense of self-discipline that is difficult to maintain (at least this author finds it such!). There are several strategies to consider. A manager could prepare an individual development plan as part of a formal HR process or as an informal, personal initiative and identify management knowledge skills that he or she needs to acquire or update. In preparing the plan, the manager would locate appropriate workshops, seminars, or academic courses to address professional needs. Thoughtfully planned on a yearly basis, this strategy helps the archival manager to keep sharp and on top of management challenges.

Another strategy involves the archival manager as educator. Teaching management workshops or courses within the institution, in archival programs at local colleges and universities, or for professional associations requires study and preparation that will benefit the manager on the job. This is a more taxing strategy but potentially has long-term benefits. Whatever strategy is adopted, keeping up with professional literature is a requirement. Hopefully, the journals and publications described in the appendix provide fertile possibilities.

The final point is that the archival manager is not alone. Managers work in such complex professional environments that it is impossible to master all the professional knowledge needed to be a successful manager. Networking with other professionals to gain their expertise and help is absolutely essential. Information professionals increasingly interdepend on each other and on other professionals as well. The archival manager does not need to master everything but does need to know what help is needed to get the job done. Perhaps the image of the archival manager as the happy, skillful networker is just the right note on which to conclude this manual.

MICHAEL J. KURTZ
March 2004

Index

Boldface indicates figures and tables.

About the Author

Michael J. Kurtz has worked at the National Archives and Records Administration for more than 30 years. He is currently Assistant Archivist for Records Services–Washington, D.C. He is a long-time member of the Society of American Archivists (SAA), where he served as chair for 10 years of the Archives Management Roundtable and also on the Committee on Education and Professional Development.